THE COMPLETE GUIDE TO
Dinosaurs
AND PREHISTORIC REPTILES

This edition published in 2012 by
CHARTWELL BOOKS, INC.
A division of BOOK SALES, INC.
276 Fifth Avenue Suite 206
New York, New York 10001
USA

Copyright © 2006 Marshall Editions
Conceived, edited, and designed by Marshall Editions
The Old Brewery, 6 Blundell Street, London N7 9BH, UK
www.quarto.com

Publisher: Richard Green
Commissioning editor: Claudia Martin
Art direction: Ivo Marloh
Editor: Johanna Geary
Design concept: Tall Tree
Design: Melissa Alaverdy
Indexer: Vanessa Bird
Production: Nikki Ingram

ISBN 13: 978-0-7858-2915-7

Originated in Hong Kong by Modern Age
Printed and bound in China by Hung Hing

2 4 6 8 10 9 7 5 3 1

THE COMPLETE GUIDE TO
Dinosaurs
AND PREHISTORIC REPTILES

Chris McNab
Consultant: Professor Michael Benton

CHARTWELL
BOOKS, INC.

Contents

Introduction

Millions of years before the first humans emerged, life on Earth was dominated by dinosaurs and other amazing reptiles. Thriving in the prehistoric seas, skies, and on land, they ruled the Earth for 165 million years. This book looks at the development of these fascinating creatures, and the changing world in which they lived.

The Changing Globe

The Earth hasn't always looked like it does today. Throughout our planet's long history, the shapes of the continents, the depths of the oceans, the climate, and the animals that live on Earth have changed dramatically. The reason for many of these changes has been the constant, but slow, movement of tectonic plates—large pieces of the Earth's surface. Over hundreds of millions of years, the flow of hot rocky material underneath the Earth's surface has caused these plates to move thousands of miles. When one plate collides with another, it can push land and ocean sediment upwards, creating a mountain range. The collisions can also cause earthquakes or volcanic eruptions. These natural disasters can change the Earth's climate, making the air warmer or cooler, or raising or lowering the level of the sea. Some plants and animals will thrive in the new environment, while others die out.

Carboniferous Period
The southern continents that made up a great land mass called Gondwana moved clockwise. The eastern part (India, Australia, and Antarctica) moved south and the western part (South America and Africa) moved north.

Permian Period
The Earth's plates moved together to form a supercontinent called Pangaea. This landmass stretched from pole to pole and included North America, Europe, North Asia, Africa, South America, India, Australia, and Antarctica.

Triassic Period
Pangaea continued to dominate the Earth. Because the landmasses were all joined to each other, plants and animals could spread across the world easily. The climate was warm and there were no polar ice caps.

Jurassic Period
Pangaea split into two, creating two land areas: Laurasia in the north and Gondwana in the south. The climate was still warm all over the world, but the amount of rain that fell had increased.

Cretaceous Period
The continents had drifted close to where they are today. As the land broke into smaller pieces, greater differences between the dinosaurs in different areas developed as they adapted to their changing environments.

Tertiary Period
Australia separated from Antarctica, and India joined with Asia. By five million years ago, the world appeared much as it does now. North and South America became joined by a land bridge as sea levels fell.

How to Use this Book

This encyclopedia is divided into two chapters: "Early Life on Earth" and "Dinosaurs and Other Early Reptiles." The first chapter describes the beginnings of our planet and the first life forms that emerged. The second chapter introduces you to all the types of dinosaurs and early reptiles, with illustrations and facts about different species. There are also special double-page features that look in more detail at life on Earth during particular moments of its prehistory, and at different aspects of dinosaur life.

Therizinosaurus

Scale
The silhouettes compare the size of the animal with an average adult human.

Period
The letters show the period or epoch in which the animal lived. The key is below.

Size
The approximate size of the animal is given in imperial and metric measurements.

Order
This gives the order to which the family belongs.

Family
This gives the family to which the species belongs.

Map
This shows what the Earth looked like at the time the animal lived. The red dots indicate the areas that the species inhabited.

Range
This lists the areas of the world in which fossils of the species have been found.

Pronunciation
This explains how to say the animal's name. Capital letters (SAW) show that this part of the word should be stressed.

Cr	Late Cretaceous

Size: 13-16 ft/4-5 m long

Order: Saurischia

Family: Therizinosauridae

Range: Asia: Mongolia and China

Pronunciation: thair-uh-ZEEN-uh-SAW-rus

Period Chart

Eon	Era	Period	Epoch	Date at Beginning (mya)
Precambrian eon				4,560
Phanerozoic eon	Palaeozoic era	Cambrian period		542
		Ordovician period		488
		Silurian period		444
		Devonian period		416
		Carboniferous period		359
		Permian period		299
	Mesozoic era	Triassic period		251
		Jurassic period		200
		Cretaceous period		145
		Tertiary period	Palaeocene epoch	65
			Eocene epoch	56
			Oligocene epoch	34
			Miocene epoch	23
			Pliocene epoch	5
	Cenozoic era	Quaternary period	Pleistocene epoch	1.8
			Holocene epoch	0.01

The history of the Earth is divided into two major eons: the Precambrian and the Phanerozoic. The Precambrian is the longest, spanning the time from the Earth's origins to the beginnings of life. The Phanerozoic eon dates from the time when life began to thrive on Earth and includes three eras: the Palaeozoic, Mesozoic, and Cenozoic. These are in turn divided into periods and epochs. The dates on the chart show how many millions of years ago (mya) each began.

Key to Symbols

Ca
Carboniferous
359 to 299 mya

Pe
Permian
299 to 251 mya

Tr
Triassic
251 to 200 mya

Ju
Jurassic
200 to 145 mya

Cr
Cretaceous
145 to 65 mya

Eo
Eocene
56 to 34 mya

Pli
Pliocene
5 to 1.8 mya

Ple
Pleistocene
1.8 mya to 10,000 years ago

EARLY LIFE ON EARTH

T he Earth itself is 4.5 billion years old. Scientists think the planet was formed when gas and dust were thrown together following the "Big Bang." For the first billion years, there was no life at all on the planet. The world was baking hot and covered in poisonous gases. However, slowly the land and seas took shape, and the atmosphere we breathe today emerged. It was now a planet that could support life.

The first life developed in the oceans. It began with tiny, microscopic organisms smaller than a pin head. Over millions of years, some of these organisms developed into soft-bodied sea creatures. By 500 million years ago, creatures with backbones were swimming about in the oceans. Then, around 360 million years ago, amphibians appeared. These were creatures that could live in water and on the land. Slowly, four-legged animal life started to spread onto solid ground.

The earliest reptiles developed about 300 million years ago. Reptiles lay hard-shelled eggs which can survive outside water, unlike the jelly-covered eggs of amphibians. Reptiles' limbs were well suited to moving about on land. From the small early reptiles grew the mighty dinosaurs that were to rule the Earth for 150 million years.

Birth of Our Planet

The early history of the Earth is a story of slow but amazing change. At first the Earth was a red-hot, fiery ball. In time, however, its surface cooled and the first signs of life emerged. These life forms were tiny, but over millions of years they grew into the creatures of the dinosaur age.

Right: There were about 8 billion years between the "Big Bang" that created the Universe to the moment life began on Earth. It would take another 3 billion years for complex organisms to appear.

Below: The "Big Bang" was a vast explosion that happened about 12 billion years ago. It threw out the material that would eventually make up the Universe.

The planets may have been formed by pieces of dust and rock crashing into one another and joining together.

The Big Bang

Following a huge explosion, called the "Big Bang," massive pieces of rock and ice, along with dust and gas, all joined together to form the Earth. As these pieces collided 4.6 billion years ago, they gave out an enormous amount of heat, warming the Earth up to a temperature of 9,000°F (5,000°C).

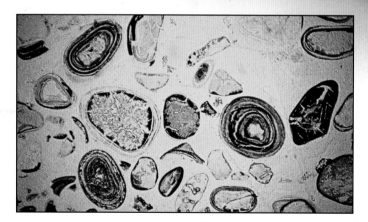

Above: The gunflint chert rocks pictured here show some of the earliest examples of life on our planet. They contain microscopic fossils of different bacteria that lived about 1.9 billion years ago.

After the collision came a "meltdown" that lasted 100 million years. During this time, the Earth's interior formed. Heavy iron and nickel minerals sank down to create a hot, dense core 4,400 miles (7,080 km) across. Lighter minerals moved to the surface and formed a rocky outer crust about 4.5 billion years ago. Between the core and the crust, a mass of hot rock 1,800 miles (2,900 km) thick was formed. This is called the mantle. Heat still moves upwards from the middle of the Earth today—causing volcanic eruptions and earthquakes.

Land, Sea, and Life

Large volcanic eruptions of gas and steam helped to make the early atmosphere and the first bodies of water on Earth. Scientists are still not sure how the land—also called the continental crust—came about. The lighter rocks of the crust may have risen high enough to form land "islands." These islands probably then joined together to make the first large areas of land. By 4 billion years ago, the crust had cooled and tiny life forms began to appear.

Below: About 4.5 billion years ago, it is thought that a planet the size of Mars may have crashed into the Earth.

Above: The Moon may have formed from pieces of the Earth thrown out after the collision.

Scientists argue today about how life began. One of the basic parts of living things is something called amino acids. In the early 1950s, a scientist at the University of Chicago showed that it was possible to make amino acids with just a simple atmosphere, some water, and a few flashes of lightning. Other scientists think that life began when the Earth's surface was hit by meteorites from outer space about 4 billion years ago. They believe that the meteorites carried the beginnings of life in them. However life began, the first tiny organisms had to survive extreme conditions. There was no oxygen (the gas we need to breathe) and no protection from the Sun's scorching rays.

Below: About 3.5 billion years ago, the Earth had cooled enough for oceans and an early atmosphere to form.

Life Begins

The oldest known fossils on Earth have been found in rocks that are about 3.5 billion years old. The earliest form of life on Earth was bacteria. Today we mostly hear about bacteria because it can cause diseases. Billions of years ago, however, bacteria brought life to the world.

Early Bacteria

The early organisms on Earth were very basic indeed. They were nothing like the plants and creatures we see today, which developed millions and millions of years later. Microscopic bacteria were the first living things—or organisms—to exist on Earth. These tiny life forms were able to live in a very tough place. Temperatures were very hot, and there was no oxygen in the atmosphere. How did they survive? Scientists have found some clues in the world today.

The springwaters of Yellowstone National Park in Wyoming are home to "thermophilic" bacteria. These organisms live in water as hot as 185°F (85°C)—that's almost boiling temperature. On the other hand, "psychrophile" bacteria prefer to live in Antarctic sea-ice, where the water is very cold. Other bacteria can survive in water that is full of dangerous acids. Another discovery came from the bottom of the ocean. There scientists found hot jets of water coming out of the seabed. Around these jets were bacteria.

Above: In warm shallow seas, such as Mexico's Sea of Cortez, structures called stromatolites are being built. They are made today exactly as they were by early life forms billions of years ago. Sediments and bacteria join together to form the strange mounds.

Volcanic hills

Stromatolites

Seabed sediment

These bacteria could reproduce—make new bacteria—even at the depths of the ocean, without any sunlight at all, and they could survive in temperatures of over 212°F (100°C).

All of these forms of bacteria belong to the most primitive group of organisms known, the Archaebacteria. These bacteria can survive without oxygen or light. Among the earliest fossils are the stromatolites. The first stromatolites are over 3 billion years old. Stromatolites were built by a blue-green bacteria called algae. The algae at first formed in mats on the seabed. The mats were covered in sediment—layers of dirt and rock. Because of this, the algae had to grow upwards through the dirt. Over time it built itself up into a mound up to 3 ft (1 m) high and 1 ft (30 cm) wide. Mounds of algae are still created in the same way today in warm tropical waters. The mounds are easily preserved as fossils.

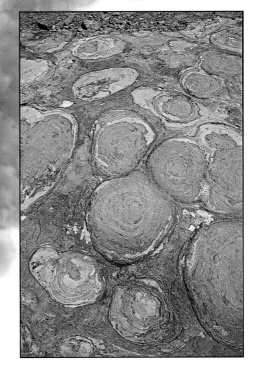

Above: These stromatolite fossils are billions of years old. They were found in the Glacier National Park, Montana.

Below: By 3.5 billion years ago, algae had grown along the edges of shallow, warm seas. The algae made mats over the surface of the seabed. When these mats were covered by sediment, the organisms grew upwards. Eventually a mound of algae would be created. These mounds would have been the only visible signs of life in the period known as the Precambrian.

Volcanic eruption

In the Oceans

Life on Earth began in the oceans. Tiny organisms developed there and evolved over millions of years into larger and more complex life forms. Simple, soft-bodied creatures were living on the planet by around 620 million years ago. These first creatures had no backbones, what we call invertebrates. By around 500 million years ago, vertebrates—animals with backbones—were swimming around the world's oceans.

Complex Organisms Emerge

The first life forms on Earth were very basic, made of just one cell. In the 1940s, scientists found the earliest fossils of many-celled life forms, in South Australia. Paleontologists named these fascinating fossils "Ediacaran" fossils, after the Ediacara Hills in Australia where they were first discovered. Hundreds of Ediacaran fossils have now been discovered in sandy rocks all over the world, from Siberia to Africa. They date from the late Precambrian era, around 620 million years ago. Ediacarans came in lots of different shapes and sizes. There were blobs, wavy stripes, and ribbons. The fossils can be as short as 0.4 in (1 cm) or as long as 3 ft 4 in (1 m). The Ediacarans were soft-bodied creatures that did not have hard parts, such as backbones or shells. Some scientists think that the Ediacarans were the ancestors of today's invertebrates—animals without backbones—such as jellyfish.

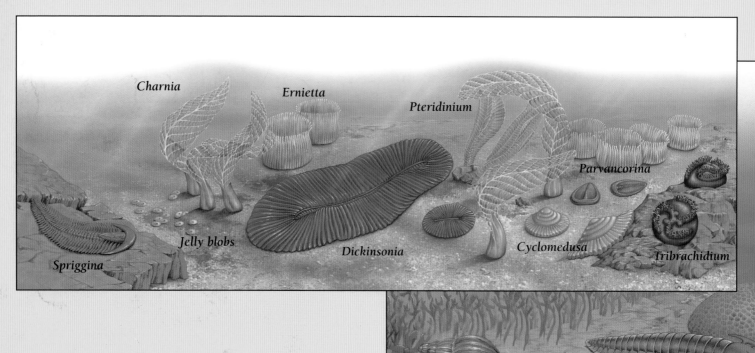

Charnia

Ernietta

Pteridinium

Parvancorina

Jelly blobs

Dickinsonia

Cyclomedusa

Tribrachidium

Spriggina

Triarthru

The First Shells

The first shelled animals developed about 540 million years ago. Some of these shelled animals belonged to a group of creatures called mollusks. Mollusks today include snails and mussels. Why did these early animals grow shells? The shells may have been needed for protection from other creatures. But scientists are not sure what exactly these tiny organisms were protecting themselves against. It is possible that the shells were used to store energy, or to make the creatures' soft, light body parts heavier, so that they did not float in the sea water.

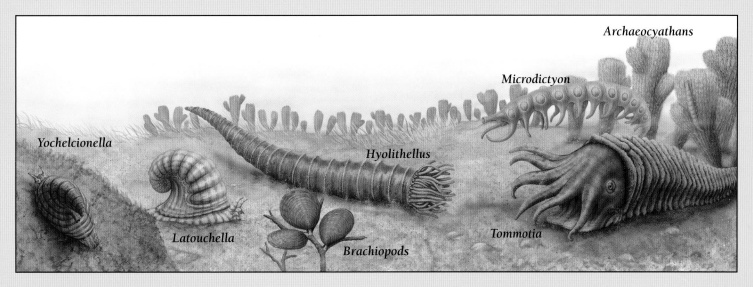

The First Vertebrates

The earliest vertebrates—animals with backbones—appeared over 500 million years ago. These organisms, called agnathans, were fishlike creatures. They did not have jaws or teeth, so they must have fed on food that was small and in good supply, such as plankton (microscopic animals and plants). The first animals with jaws emerged around 450 million years ago. These were sharklike creatures, with teeth and strong backbones.

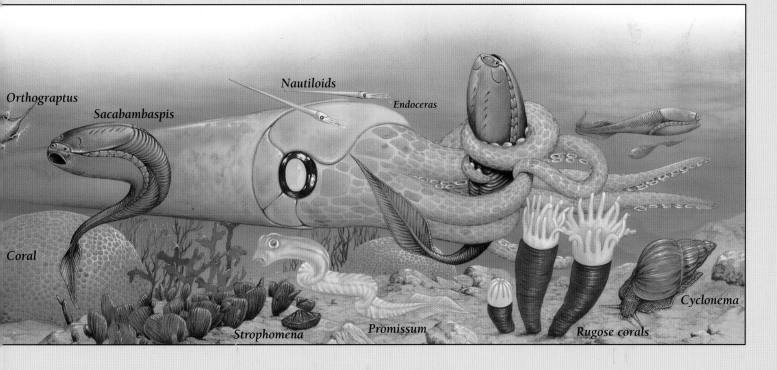

Invasion of the Land

As animals slowly began to leave the water and move onto the land, their bodies went through dramatic changes. Over millions of years, fins developed into strong legs to lift the body, and gills were replaced by air-breathing lungs so that creatures could survive in their new environment.

Above: The mudskipper is a modern fish that can leave the water to find food on mudbanks. It uses its long, bony fins to prop itself up and wriggle across soft, wet mud. However, it has to remain wet and cannot stay out of the water for long.

First Steps Toward Life on Land

The earliest fossil of a four-legged creature, called a tetrapod, was found in Greenland. It is around 360 million years old. Paleontologists think the fossil was of an animal similar to a modern salamander, able to crawl out of the water and walk on land. The creature was called *Ichthyostega*. It seems to have had the limbs and lungs of a walking, air-breathing creature, but it still had many fishlike features. Scientists think that the limbs of *Ichthyostega* were still better suited to

Gymnosperms and ferns

Balanerpton woodi

Lungfish

Early Tetrapod: Acanthostega

Acanthostega is one of the earliest known tetrapods. It had many fishlike features, such as a long, flat tail that was good for swimming, and gills for breathing underwater. But it also had what seem to be land-living features, like its four legs and a large rib cage for holding big lungs. However, scientists now think that *Acanthostega*'s limbs were actually used for walking in shallow fast-flowing streams rather than for walking on land. The limbs could also have been used for swimming. The front limbs could have held onto underwater plant roots and been used to search for food.

swimming than walking. It still had gills and may have breathed in both air and water. Creatures like *Ichthyostega* were making the difficult move from water to land, and their bodies had to adapt to their new world. *Ichthyostega* appears to fill the gap in evolution between fish and animals that lived on land.

Below: Fossils found in East Kirkton in Scotland give us a remarkable look into the Early Carboniferous period. A tropical forest covered the slopes of volcanoes and small lakes were full of creatures adapting to life on land. Lungfish had gills as well as air-breathing lungs, and the tetrapod *Westlothiana*, able to lay eggs outside of the water, was beginning to develop some reptile-like features.

Westlothiana lizziae

Millipede

Harvestman

Pulmonoscorpius

The First Reptiles

The First Reptiles

Speedy little *Hylonomus* was one of the first reptiles and one of the earliest of all land animals. It was only about 8 in (20 cm) long and had a lizard-like body and a slender tail. *Hylonomus* lived in North America more than 300 million years ago.

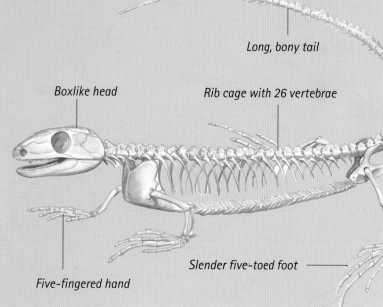

Long, bony tail

Boxlike head

Rib cage with 26 vertebrae

Slender five-toed foot

Five-fingered hand

A Shelled Egg

An amphibian egg has to be laid in water. It has no shell, only a jelly-like coating which has to be kept moist. Reptile eggs can be laid on land. They have a tough shell that protects the growing baby inside and keeps the egg from drying out. Unlike amphibians, reptile embryos feed off a yolk sac inside the egg.

Amphibian egg

Jelly coating

Embryo

Reptile egg

Yolk sac

Tough shell

Embryo

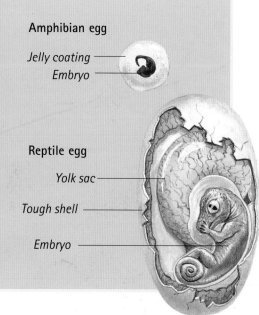

The first reptiles appeared about 300 million years ago, during the Late Carboniferous period. They evolved from amphibians—creatures like frogs and salamanders that spent at least part of their lives in water. Reptiles were the first vertebrates (animals with backbones) to live entirely on land. Unlike amphibians, reptiles did not need the water to breed and could lay hard-shelled eggs on shore. The early reptiles were small creatures that the insects or spiders, which they snapped up with their small, sharp teeth. The very first reptiles were called anapsids. They had heavy boxlike skulls with openings only for the eyes and nostrils. Later came diapsid and synapsid reptiles. These had lighter skulls with extra openings and much stronger jaw muscles, which helped them to bite with more power.

Types of Early Reptile

Mammal-like reptiles: Dicynodon
The first mammal-like reptiles lived some 300 million years ago. They were the biggest, fiercest land animals on Earth before the appearance of the dinosaurs. But they were all extinct by the middle of the Jurassic period.

Early Reptiles: Hylonomus
The first reptiles, such as *Hylonomus*, belonged to a group called anapsids and had boxlike skulls. They evolved during the Late Carboniferous period.

Crocodiles: Teleosaurus
Crocodiles lived at the same time as dinosaurs and they have hardly changed to this day. They have tough bodies, short legs, and long tails. They are very fierce hunters.

Ichthyosaur: Stenopterygius
Ichthyosaurs were marine reptiles that had adapted to life in the sea. They were shaped much like dolphins today and could swim fast as they hunted for fish and squid.

Lizards: Ardeosaurus
The first lizards lived in the mid-Jurassic period, about 175 million years ago. There are still lots of different kinds of lizards in the world today that look a lot like *Ardeosaurus*.

Turtles: Archelo
Turtles, which are anapsids like the very earliest reptiles, first appeared in the Late Triassic period 220 million years ago. Triassic turtles had hard shells, just like turtles and tortoises today.

Flying Reptiles: Pteranodon
Pterosaurs evolved in the Late Triassic period 220 million years ago. They were the first creatures to take to life in the air. They flew on wings made of skin, which were attached to their long finger bones and their legs.

Birth of the Dinosaurs

Dinosaurs, or "ruling reptiles," were the most amazing reptiles that have ever lived. The first dinosaurs emerged during the Late Triassic period, about 225 million years ago. The biggest dinosaurs were more than 100 ft (30 m) long, some of the most gigantic creatures to ever walk the Earth. Others were tiny, birdlike creatures. They lived on land, laid eggs with hard shells, and had strong skeletons and thick leathery skin. There are at least 500 known kinds of dinosaur, but there may be many more that have not yet been discovered. After ruling the Earth for more than 150 million years, the dinosaurs mysteriously died out at the end of the Cretaceous period, about 65 million years ago.

Ways of Moving

Early reptiles moved with their legs sprawled out to the sides, like lizards do today. Dinosaurs had a more efficient way of moving. Their legs were straight underneath their bodies. This meant that they could carry more weight and move faster, with longer strides.

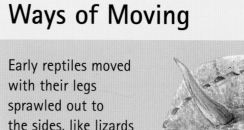

Dinosaur

Lizard

Two Dinosaur Orders

There were two groups of dinosaurs—ornithischians, which fed on plants, and saurischians, which included meat-eaters and plant-eaters. The main difference between the two groups was in their hip bones. Saurischian dinosaurs had a pubis bone that pointed away from the ischium bone. In ornithischian dinosaurs, the pubis bone was below the ischium bone.

A skeleton of the saurischian dinosaur *Ornitholestes*

A skeleton of the ornithischian dinosaur *Iguanodon*

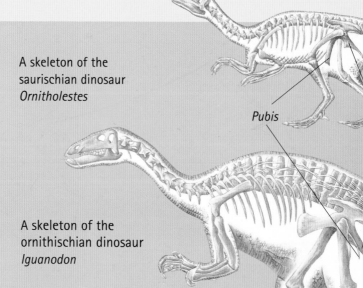

Pubis

Ischium

Types of Dinosaurs

SAURISCHIANS

Carnosaurs
This group included some of the best known of all dinosaurs—the tyrannosaurs and hunters such as *Allosaurus*. They were all large creatures with big heads and jaws lined with deadly, razor-sharp teeth.

Ornithomimids
These dinosaurs looked very like the ostriches of today. They could run fast on their long back legs.

Dromaeosaurs
Dromaeosaurs were fast runners too, but were much fiercer than ornithomimids. They had a lethal claw on each foot, which they could use as weapons.

Coelurosaurs
These were fast-moving hunters with slender legs and strong claws on their hands and feet.

Sauropods
These huge, long-necked plant-eaters were the giants of the dinosaur world. They included mighty creatures such as *Brachiosaurus*, *Diplodocus*, and *Seismosaurus*. The biggest were well over 50 ft (15 m) long.

ORNITHISCHIANS

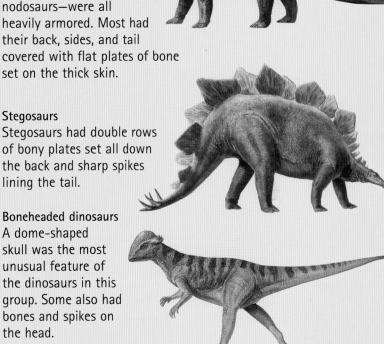

Armored dinosaurs
The dinosaurs in this group—ankylosaurs and nodosaurs—were all heavily armored. Most had their back, sides, and tail covered with flat plates of bone set on the thick skin.

Stegosaurs
Stegosaurs had double rows of bony plates set all down the back and sharp spikes lining the tail.

Boneheaded dinosaurs
A dome-shaped skull was the most unusual feature of the dinosaurs in this group. Some also had bones and spikes on the head.

Horned dinosaurs
These dinosaurs had heavily armored bodies with huge curving horns on the head and a sheet of bone curving out from the back of the skull.

Duckbilled dinosaurs
Duckbills were among the most common dinosaurs. All had beaklike snouts and most had horns or crests on their heads.

Iguanodons
These large plant-eating dinosaurs had a sharp thumb spike on each hand. This could be bent across the palm for holding food.

DINOSAURS
AND OTHER EARLY
REPTILES

One hundred million years before the dinosaurs appeared, early reptiles took over the land. Unlike the mighty dinosaurs, these reptiles were at first mostly small creatures, like modern lizards. Some fed on insects and spiders, which they snapped up with small, sharp teeth. Others ate the plant life that covered the planet in lush growth. Very slowly, some of the early reptiles evolved into the most powerful beasts ever to walk the face of the Earth—the dinosaurs.

Dinosaurs were reptiles—the word dinosaur actually means "terrible lizard." They came in an amazing variety of shapes and sizes. The smallest dinosaurs were about the same size as a chicken. The largest dinosaurs, such as *Sauroposeidon*, could grow to 102 ft (31 m) long and weighed 59 U.S. tons (53.5 tonnes). The dinosaurs also had different behaviors. Some were plant-eaters and lived in large herds, whereas others lived mostly alone and hunted other dinosaurs. Scientists have identified at least 500 different kinds of dinosaurs, but there may have been many more that no one knows about yet. Much about these incredible creatures remains a mystery.

Early Reptiles

Before reptiles, there were reptiliomorphs. These were like reptiles in many ways, but had important differences in their limbs and bones. Some scientists think that reptiliomorphs are the link between the earliest four-footed animals—called tetrapods—and true reptiles. The first proper reptiles emerged about 300 million years ago, in a time now known as the Carboniferous period. Unlike amphibians, which live mostly in water, the reptiles had limbs perfect for moving on solid ground. They also found plenty of food on the land, and so became one of the planet's most successful life forms.

Labidosaurus

This heavy, strong reptile had a large head and a short tail. Its powerful limbs suggest that it could survive easily on the land. *Labidosaurus* had several rows of very sharp teeth in its jaws. By having lots of teeth, *Labidosaurus* would find it easy to crush up shelled creatures such as snails. It could also grind up tough plant material.

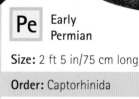

Labidosaurus

Pe	Early Permian
Size: 2 ft 5 in/75 cm long	
Order: Captorhinida	
Family: Captorhinidae	
Range: North America: Texas	
Pronunciation: la-BID-oh-SAW-rus	

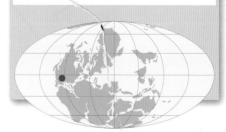

Westlothiana

The fossils of *Westlothiana* were first found in 1984. The creature, which was nicknamed "Lizzie the lizard," dates back about 340 million years. It is the oldest known reptiliomorph. Unlike the amphibians, from which it developed, it could lay eggs with hard outer shells. This meant that it could breed on the land.

Ca	Lower Carboniferous
Size: 11 in/30 cm	
Order: Reptiliomorph	
Family: Basal reptiliomorph	
Range: Scotland	
Pronunciation: west-lo-thee-AR-na	

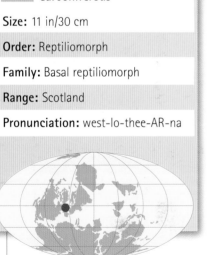

Westlothiana

Pe Late Permian

Size: 8 ft/2.5 m long

Order: Captorhinida

Family: Pareiasauridae

Range: Eastern Europe

Pronunciation: scoot-oh-SAW-rus

Scutosaurus

Scutosuarus had a massive body, a heavy, spiked head, and bony armor on its body. While many reptiles at this time walked low to the ground, *Scutosaurus* walked taller and more upright. Its legs were more directly beneath the animal's body—that way they could support the creature's great weight. This manner of walking was also seen in the later dinosaurs. Such a heavy, slow-moving animal would not be able to move great distances, so it probably stayed around local feeding grounds.

Scutosaurus

Elginia

This creature was one of the last of the pareiasaurs. Pareiasaurs were large plant-eating reptiles that grew up to 10 ft (3 m) long. *Elginia*, however, was one of the smallest. Its head had bony spikes. These were probably used more for display than for fighting.

Elginia

Pe Late Permian

Size: 2 ft/60 cm long

Order: Captorhinida

Family: Pareiasauridae

Range: Europe: Scotland

Pronunciation: el-GIN-ee-a

25

Life in Carboniferous Nova Scotia

Fossils found in underground coal at Joggins, Nova Scotia, in Canada, have given us a picture of life in a Carboniferous swamp. Plants such as horsetail and clubmosses covered the banks in a thick, green carpet. For the early reptiles living in this damp, tropical world, these plants and millions of large insects provided food.

An amazing find at the Joggins site were the many tree stumps and trunks preserved in the earth. More than 190 fossil skeletons of small amphibians have been found in about 30 tree-sized stumps. Even more surprising, inside these stumps were the fossils of some of the oldest known egg-laying reptiles. These were called *Hylonomus lyelli* and *Paleothyris*.

These first reptiles were small—about 8 in (20 cm) long. They looked rather like the insect-eating lizards we see today.

They probably hatched from a tiny egg about ½ in (1 cm) across. Such creatures were able to live on land because they found plenty of food there, which they could eat with small, sharp teeth. On the menu were millipedes, spiders, flies, and other insects.

Charcoal was often found within the stumps and in the surrounding earth. Charcoal is made when wood is burnt, and at Joggins the charcoal came from forest fires. The animals found at

Clubmosses

Hylonomus

Horsetails

Carboniferous Reptile: Hylonomus

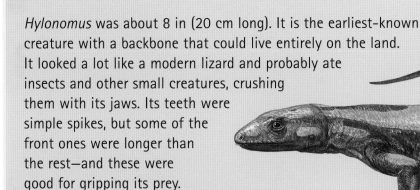

Hylonomus was about 8 in (20 cm long). It is the earliest-known creature with a backbone that could live entirely on the land. It looked a lot like a modern lizard and probably ate insects and other small creatures, crushing them with its jaws. Its teeth were simple spikes, but some of the front ones were longer than the rest—and these were good for gripping its prey.

The fossil bones of *Hylonomus* were found in the coal beds of Nova Scotia. Some *Hylonomus* died in the holes left by rotted giant clubmosses, which they had probably explored in search of insect food.

Joggins may have tried to find shelter in the trunks, only to suffocate and die. On the other hand, the creatures may have simply lived in the stumps, or fell into the stumps, became trapped, and eventually died. Whatever the case, Joggins has been an amazing find for paleontologists.

Hylonomus in clubmoss stump

Mammal-like Reptiles

Some early reptiles, known as the synapsids, developed a different-shaped skull and much more powerful jaws. The jaws of the synapsids could be opened wide and snapped shut to kill large prey. These reptiles are known as the mammal-like reptiles, because they are the ancestors of today's mammals. The first mammal-like reptiles, the pelycosaurs, were seen during the Late Carboniferous period, some 300 million years ago. The pelycosaurs started as small, lizard-like creatures, but they evolved into many different creatures that were larger, heavier, and stronger. Some were plant-eaters (known as herbivores), while others ate meat (carnivores).

Pe	Early Permian
Size: 5 ft/1.5 m long	
Order: Pelycosauria	
Family: Varanopseidae	
Range: North America: Texas	
Pronunciation: va-ran-oh-SAW-rus	

Varanosaurus

Varanosaurus lived in the same place at the same time as *Ophiacodon* (opposite). They probably fought over fish in the same swamps. Its skull was deep and narrow, and the long jaws were armed with small, needle-like teeth. It looked a lot like a lizard still alive today, called the monitor lizard.

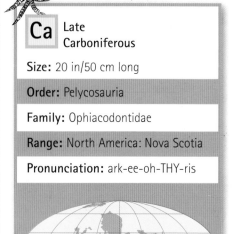

Archaeothyris

Archaeothyris

This small, lizard-like creature is the earliest-known pelycosaur. Its remains were found in North America. At the time it lived, the climate was warm and damp. Great forests of conifers and ferns and mosses covered the land. *Archaeothyris'* jaws were very strong. Although its teeth were all the same shape—sharp and pointed—they were of different sizes. Such teeth suggest it ate a carnivorous diet.

Ca	Late Carboniferous
Size: 20 in/50 cm long	
Order: Pelycosauria	
Family: Ophiacodontidae	
Range: North America: Nova Scotia	
Pronunciation: ark-ee-oh-THY-ris	

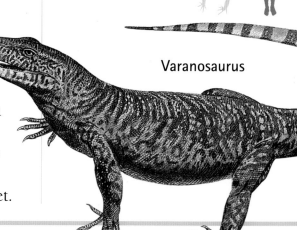
Varanosaurus

Ophiacodon

Ophiacodon had a skull with a deep, narrow shape. This shape meant that it could have long and very strong jaw muscles. Its back legs were longer than its front legs, so it was probably a good runner, even though it was much larger than the earlier pelycosaurs. It weighed between 66 lb and 110 lb (30 kg and 50 kg). To take the weight off its feet, it is likely that *Ophiacodon* spent some of its time in shallow water. There it scuttled about in floodplains or swamps, catching fish and amphibians in its jaws, and killing them with its sharp teeth.

Pe	Early Permian
Size: up to 12 ft/3.6 m long	
Order: Pelycosauria	
Family: Ophiacodontidae	
Range: North America: Texas	
Pronunciation: off-ee-AK-o-don	

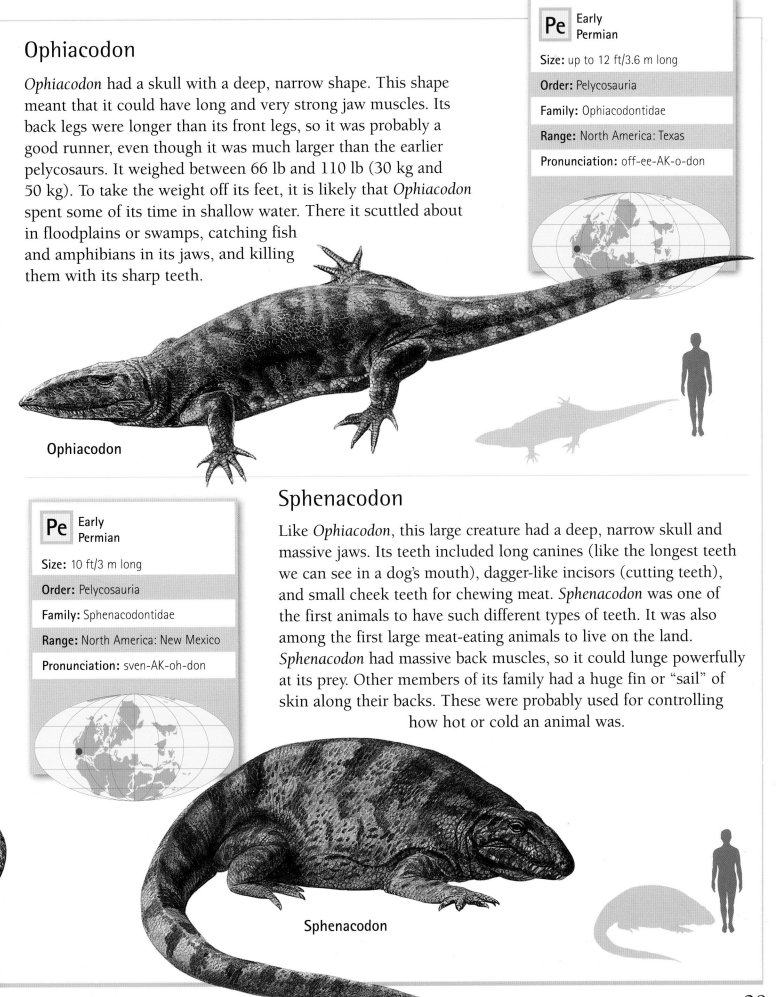

Ophiacodon

Sphenacodon

Pe	Early Permian
Size: 10 ft/3 m long	
Order: Pelycosauria	
Family: Sphenacodontidae	
Range: North America: New Mexico	
Pronunciation: sven-AK-oh-don	

Like *Ophiacodon*, this large creature had a deep, narrow skull and massive jaws. Its teeth included long canines (like the longest teeth we can see in a dog's mouth), dagger-like incisors (cutting teeth), and small cheek teeth for chewing meat. *Sphenacodon* was one of the first animals to have such different types of teeth. It was also among the first large meat-eating animals to live on the land. *Sphenacodon* had massive back muscles, so it could lunge powerfully at its prey. Other members of its family had a huge fin or "sail" of skin along their backs. These were probably used for controlling how hot or cold an animal was.

Sphenacodon

Dimetrodon

The large "sail" on the back of *Dimetrodon* has earned it the nickname of "finback." The sail was made up of long spines that came out of the animal's backbone. Across this frame was stretched a wide sheet of skin. The sail could be up to 3 ft 3 in (1 m) long in the middle. In the morning, a *Dimetrodon* would stand with its sail facing toward the rising sun. The sail would take in heat from the sun, warm the animal's blood, and so warm its whole body. To cool down, *Dimetrodon* would angle its sail away from the sun and into the cooling wind.

Pe	Early Permian
Size:	10 ft/3 m long
Order:	Pelycosauria
Family:	Sphenacodontidae
Range:	North America: Oklahoma and Texas
Pronunciation:	die-MET-ro-don

Cistecephalus

Dicynodonts were a type of reptile with two downward-pointing tusks. Some liked to spend a lot of time in the water. Others looked in the forests for food. *Cistecephalus* lived underground. This creature had a wedge-shaped, flat head, a short body, and strong, stumpy front legs with wide toes, like those of a modern mole. It probably used its powerful limbs to dig into the soil to find worms.

Cistecephalus

Pe	Late Permian
Size:	13 in/33 cm long
Order:	Therapsida
Suborder:	Dicynodontidae
Range:	Africa: South Africa
Pronunciation:	sist-e-SEF-a-lus

Dimetrodon

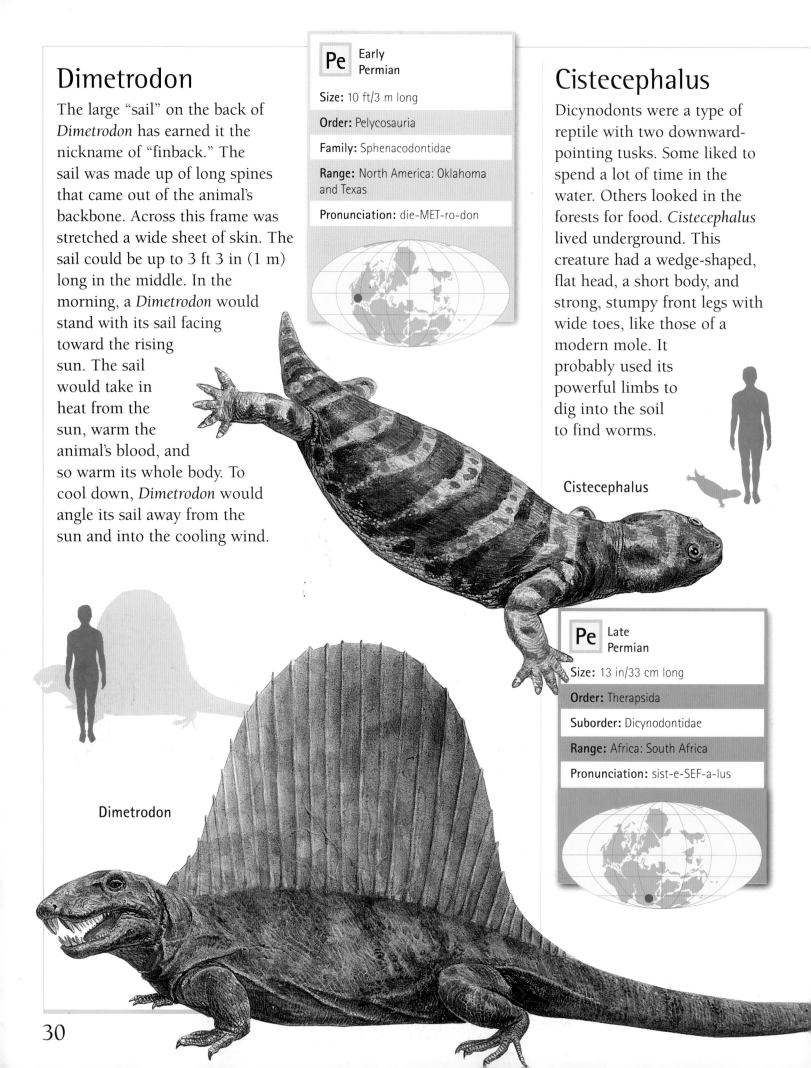

Edaphosaurus

Edaphosaurus had a large sail on its back, like *Dimetrodon*. As well as helping the animal to warm up or cool down, the sail could also have been used to attract mates or scare off predators. It may have been brightly colored. *Edaphosaurus* was a heavy, slow creature. Its body was long and shaped like a barrel. Its teeth were those of a herbivore, and were ideal for grinding up plant food.

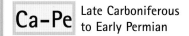

Ca–Pe	Late Carboniferous to Early Permian

Size: 10 ft/3 m long

Order: Pelycosauria

Family: Edaphosauridae

Range: Europe: Czechoslovakia; North America: Texas

Pronunciation: ee-daph-o-SAW-rus

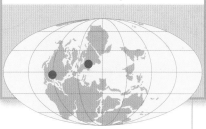

Edaphosaurus

Titanosuchus

Pe	Late Permian

Size: 8 ft/2.5 m long

Order: Therapsida

Family: Dinocephalidae

Range: Africa: South Africa

Pronunciation: ti-TAN-oh-SOOK-us

Titanosuchus was a member of a group of creatures called dinocephalians. Dinocephalian means "terrible head," as they had large skulls. *Titanosuchus* was carnivorous. Its mouth had sharp incisors and fanglike canines at the front of the jaws, and meat-shearing teeth at the back.

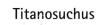

Titanosuchus

Dicynodon

Dicynodon had a powerful pair of canine tusks in its upper jaw. Scientists put this creature in a group of prehistoric creatures called dicynodonts. Dicynodont means "two dog teeth." *Dicynodon* may have used its strong tusks to dig up plants, helped by its horny beak. Apart from the tusks, *Dicynodon* had almost no other teeth. There was another group of plant-eating reptiles around at the time called pareiasaurs. These were large beasts. They had tough bodies and full sets of leaf-shaped teeth in their jaws. These two types of reptiles, with their very different teeth, ate different varieties of plant, so they didn't need to fight over food.

Tr Early Triassic

Size: 8 in/20 cm long

Order: Therapsida

Suborder: Therocephalia

Range: Africa: South Africa

Pronunciation: eric-ee-oh-LA-cherta

Ericiolacerta

Pe Late Permian

Size: 4 ft/1.2 m long

Order: Therapsida

Suborder: Dicynodontia

Range: Africa: South Africa and Tanzania

Pronunciation: die-KY-no-don

Ericiolacerta

This lizard-like creature was an insect-eater. It had small teeth and long, slim limbs, and probably moved quickly. It appeared around 240 million years ago, during the early Triassic period. At this time there was lots of plant life in Africa, where *Ericiolacerta* came from. The plants not only provided food for herbivores, but also gave homes and food to the many insects that *Ericiolacerta* fed on.

Dicynodon

Kannemeyeria

Kannemeyeria was a huge creature that grew up to 10 ft (3 m) long. Its heavy, bulky body was supported by four short, powerful legs and it had a tough hide to protect it from predators. *Kannemeyeria*'s massive head was actually quite light. This was because its skull had large openings for the eyes, nostrils, and jaw muscles. When eating, *Kannemeyeria* would tear off mouthfuls of leaves and roots. It ripped these up with its powerful, horny beak and ground them down with its toothless jaws.

Tr Early Triassic

Size: up to 10 ft/3 m long

Order: Therapsida

Suborder: Dicynodontia

Range: Africa: South Africa; Asia: India; South America: Argentina

Pronunciation: KAN-eh-MAY-er-ee-a

Kannemeyeria

Pe Late Permian

Size: 3 ft 3 in/1 m long

Order: Therapsidae

Suborder: Gorgonopsia

Range: Africa: South Africa; Russia

Pronunciation: ly-KINE-ops

Lycaenops

Lycaenops means "wolf face." It was a small, light meat-eater, with long legs for running quickly and chasing down prey. It lived in southern Africa and Russia. When hunting it probably worked in a pack. The pack would be strong enough to bring down large plant-eaters. *Lycaenops* had very long canine teeth and the front of its skull was deeper than normal to fit these teeth.

Lycaenops

33

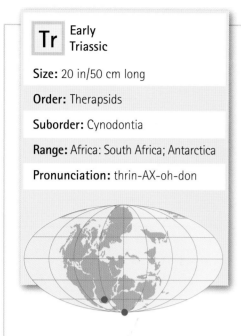

Tr	Early Triassic

Size: 20 in/50 cm long

Order: Therapsids

Suborder: Cynodontia

Range: Africa: South Africa; Antarctica

Pronunciation: thrin-AX-oh-don

Cynognathus

Thrinaxodon

Thrinaxodon looked a lot like a modern mammal. It was a small, tough carnivore. Like many other meat-eaters, *Thrinaxodon* could probably run quite fast. Its strong hind legs would help it to sprint quickly and pounce on prey. Its teeth on either side of its jaw were set into a single bone called the dentary. This single lower jaw bone was a key development of mammal-like reptiles, allowing a much stronger bite than creatures with several bones in their jaws.

Cynognathus

Cynognathus was a terrifying creature. Its crushing jaws show that it was a ferocious predator. It was strongly built, with its hind limbs placed directly beneath its body, making it very agile. Its head was more than 1 ft (30 cm) long. *Cynognathus* had a very solid lower jaw and a set of teeth designed for killing prey and eating meat. The teeth included cutting incisors, stabbing canines, and shearing cheek teeth. Its jaws were also able to open very wide, and strong muscles gave these jaws a massive bite.

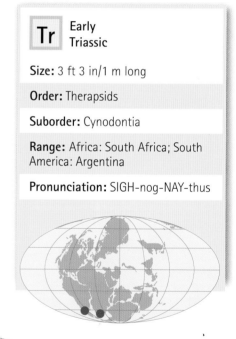

Tr	Early Triassic

Size: 3 ft 3 in/1 m long

Order: Therapsids

Suborder: Cynodontia

Range: Africa: South Africa; South America: Argentina

Pronunciation: SIGH-nog-NAY-thus

Thrinaxodon

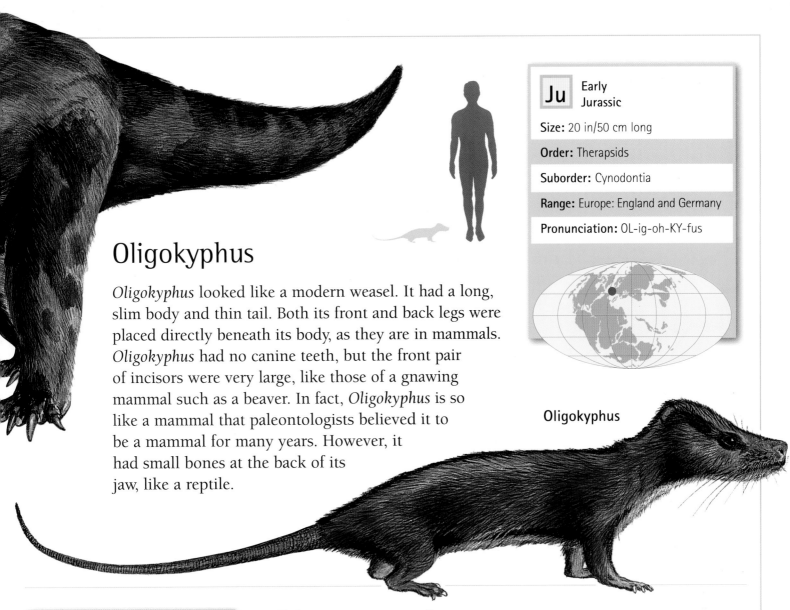

Ju	Early Jurassic
Size: 20 in/50 cm long	
Order: Therapsids	
Suborder: Cynodontia	
Range: Europe: England and Germany	
Pronunciation: OL-ig-oh-KY-fus	

Oligokyphus

Oligokyphus looked like a modern weasel. It had a long, slim body and thin tail. Both its front and back legs were placed directly beneath its body, as they are in mammals. *Oligokyphus* had no canine teeth, but the front pair of incisors were very large, like those of a gnawing mammal such as a beaver. In fact, *Oligokyphus* is so like a mammal that paleontologists believed it to be a mammal for many years. However, it had small bones at the back of its jaw, like a reptile.

Oligokyphus

Massetognathus

Tr	Middle Triassic
Size: 19 in/48 cm long	
Order: Therapsids	
Suborder: Cynodontia	
Range: South America: Argentina	
Pronunciation: MASS-e-tog-NAY-thus	

Even though it looked ferocious, *Massetognathus* was in fact a plant-eating creature. Its teeth were perfectly designed for munching through tough leaves and grasses. The teeth were large and wide for grinding up plant fibers, and the teeth of the lower jaw fitted exactly into those of the upper jaw. *Massetognathus* lived in South America in the Triassic period.

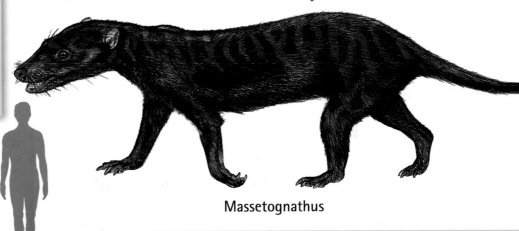

Massetognathus

35

Life in Permian South Africa

South Africa during Permian times (299–251 million years ago) was home to many reptiles and amphibians. Plant life was lush, so plant-eating reptiles were very common, such as the pig-sized *Dicynodon*. Such herbivores were hunted by carnivores like *Lycaenops*. Alongside them lived armored amphibians such as *Peltobatrachus*.

Life on Earth developed rapidly once four-legged creatures were able to lay eggs that could hatch on land. These early reptiles were known as anapsids. *Milleretta* was an anapsid reptile that lived in the Permian period. Descendants of the anapsids are today's turtles and tortoises.

Then, around 300 million years ago, the synapsid reptiles evolved. Synapsids are

Permian Early Reptile: Milleretta

Milleretta was a small, lizard-like creature. It grew to a length of around 2 ft (60 cm) and had a long tail. *Milleretta* was quick enough to chase after fast-moving insects, which it would kill with it strong jaws. It probably had very good hearing—it would use this to listen for insects moving along the ground, then chase them down when they came into sight.

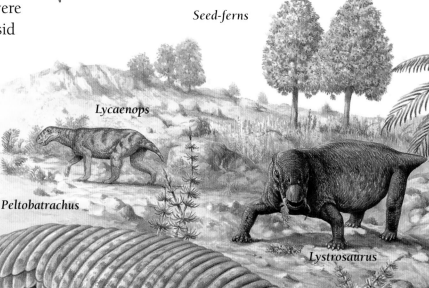

Seed-ferns

Lycaenops

Peltobatrachus

Lystrosaurus

Milleretta

Permian Mammal-like Reptile: Procynosuchus

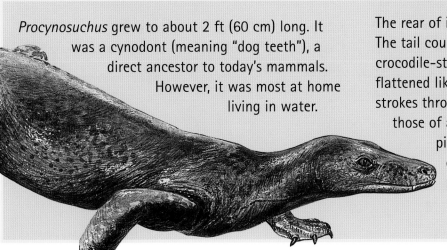

Procynosuchus grew to about 2 ft (60 cm) long. It was a cynodont (meaning "dog teeth"), a direct ancestor to today's mammals. However, it was most at home living in water.

The rear of its body and tail were very flexible. The tail could be swung from side to side, in a crocodile-style swimming motion. It was also flattened like a paddle to help it make powerful strokes through the water. Its limbs were similar to those of a modern otter. Between each toe was a piece of skin, a little like the webbed feet of a duck, and these webs were used to push against the water when *Procynosuchus* was swimming.

often called "mammal-like reptiles," because they were the ancestors of today's mammals. *Dicynodon*, *Robertia*, *Lycaenops*, and *Procynosuchus* were all Permian mammal-like reptiles. The first synapsids were called pelycosaurs. Pelycosaurs were good survivors because each creature had specialized teeth. Some became plant-eaters and others became meat-eaters.

Another group of reptiles evolved in the Late Carboniferous period, the diapsids. Modern diapsids include lizards and snakes. One of the diapsid groups, the protorosaurs, gave rise to the archosaurs, or ruling reptiles, in the Late Permian period. Dinosaurs were later members of the ruling reptile group.

Dicynodon

Robertia

Ferns

Procynosuchus

Lycaenops

Early Diapsids

Pe Early Permian

Size: 2 ft/60 m long

Order: Araeoscelidia

Family: Araeoscelididae

Range: North America: Texas

Pronunciation: AR-eye-oh-SKEL-is

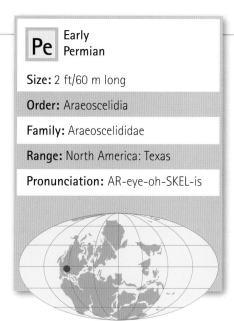

Most modern reptiles belong to the diapsid group. Diapsids first appeared in Late Carboniferous times, more than 300 million years ago. They had skulls with a pair of openings behind each eye. The muscles of the jaws were attached to ligaments that stretched across these holes. This meant that the reptiles' jaws could be opened extra wide and closed down hard to deal with large prey. The diapsids are very important in the history of the Earth. They were the ancestors of most modern reptiles (lizards, snakes, and tuataras), and the ancestors of the ruling reptiles (the dinosaurs and modern crocodiles).

Araeoscelis

Araeoscelis was similar to *Petrolacosaurus* (left), but it lived several million years later. Both animals were lizard-like creatures, with long legs for running, long necks, and small heads. The teeth of *Araeoscelis*, however, were different. Instead of the sharp, pointed teeth of *Petrolacosaurus*, *Araeoscelis* had large blunt teeth that would have been good for crushing up tough insects such as beetles.

Petrolacosaurus

The earliest-known diapsid looked a lot like a modern lizard. However, it had longer legs and a tail that was as long as its body and head put together. *Petrolacosaurus* probably also behaved like a modern lizard. It would have been a hunter, chasing around after insects. Its home was the dry, hot areas of what is now Kansas.

Ca Late Carboniferous

Size: 16 in/40 cm long

Order: Araeoscelidia

Family: Petrolacosauridae

Range: North America: Kansas

Pronunciation: PET-rol-AK-oh-SAW-rus

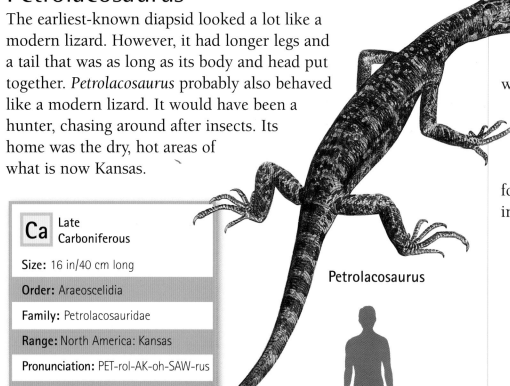

Petrolacosaurus

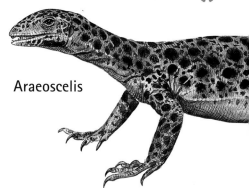

Araeoscelis

Coelurosauravus

This early reptile could glide through the air. Its ribs stretched out to each side of its short body, and flaps of skin covered the ribs to form a pair of "wings." These wings were about 1 ft (30 cm) across. *Coelurosauravus* probably lived in forests and glided from tree to tree, feeding on insects. It had a "frill" of bone at the back of its head to make it more aerodynamic.

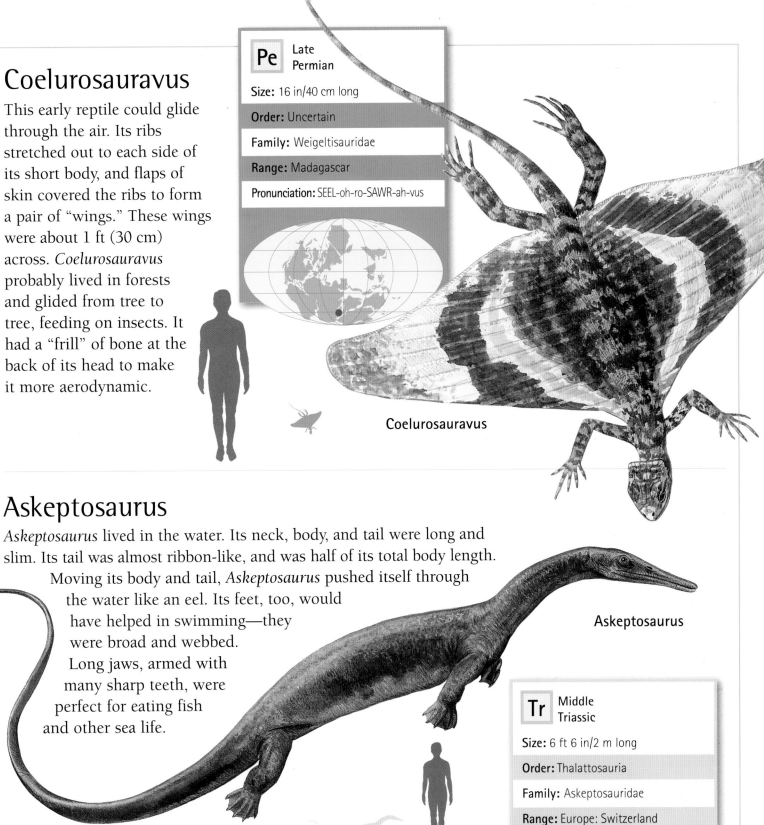

Pe	Late Permian
Size:	16 in/40 cm long
Order:	Uncertain
Family:	Weigeltisauridae
Range:	Madagascar
Pronunciation:	SEEL-oh-ro-SAWR-ah-vus

Coelurosauravus

Askeptosaurus

Askeptosaurus lived in the water. Its neck, body, and tail were long and slim. Its tail was almost ribbon-like, and was half of its total body length. Moving its body and tail, *Askeptosaurus* pushed itself through the water like an eel. Its feet, too, would have helped in swimming—they were broad and webbed. Long jaws, armed with many sharp teeth, were perfect for eating fish and other sea life.

Askeptosaurus

Tr	Middle Triassic
Size:	6 ft 6 in/2 m long
Order:	Thalattosauria
Family:	Askeptosauridae
Range:	Europe: Switzerland
Pronunciation:	a-SKEPT-o-SAW-rus

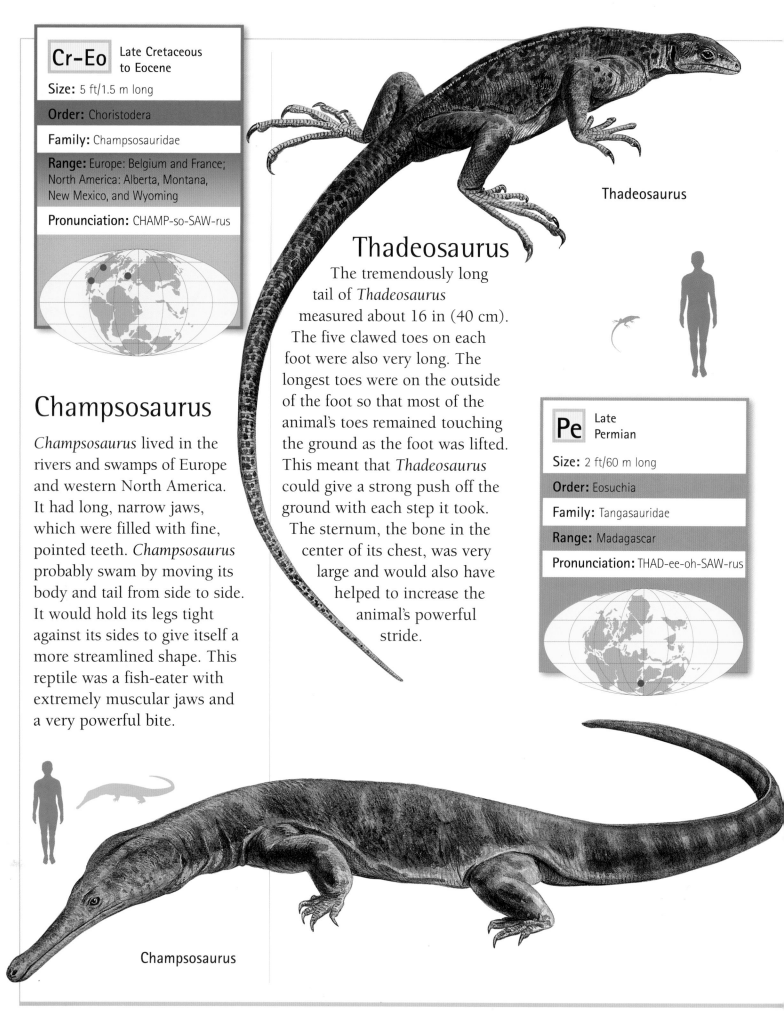

Cr–Eo Late Cretaceous to Eocene

Size: 5 ft/1.5 m long

Order: Choristodera

Family: Champsosauridae

Range: Europe: Belgium and France; North America: Alberta, Montana, New Mexico, and Wyoming

Pronunciation: CHAMP-so-SAW-rus

Thadeosaurus

Thadeosaurus

The tremendously long tail of *Thadeosaurus* measured about 16 in (40 cm). The five clawed toes on each foot were also very long. The longest toes were on the outside of the foot so that most of the animal's toes remained touching the ground as the foot was lifted. This meant that *Thadeosaurus* could give a strong push off the ground with each step it took. The sternum, the bone in the center of its chest, was very large and would also have helped to increase the animal's powerful stride.

Pe Late Permian

Size: 2 ft/60 m long

Order: Eosuchia

Family: Tangasauridae

Range: Madagascar

Pronunciation: THAD-ee-oh-SAW-rus

Champsosaurus

Champsosaurus lived in the rivers and swamps of Europe and western North America. It had long, narrow jaws, which were filled with fine, pointed teeth. *Champsosaurus* probably swam by moving its body and tail from side to side. It would hold its legs tight against its sides to give itself a more streamlined shape. This reptile was a fish-eater with extremely muscular jaws and a very powerful bite.

Champsosaurus

Planocephalosaurus

This lizard-like animal's skeleton is almost the same as that of the modern tuatara lizard that lives in New Zealand. *Planocephalosaurus* grew to only around 8 in (20 cm) long. Its teeth were very strong, and its jaws would have given a powerful bite. It would have crushed insects between its teeth, but would have also eaten worms and snails, and sometimes even small lizards.

Tr	Late Triassic
Size: 8 in/20 cm long	
Order: Sphenodontida	
Family: Sphenodontidae	
Range: Europe: England	
Pronun: PLAN-oh-KEF-al-oh-SAW-rus	

Planocephalosaurus

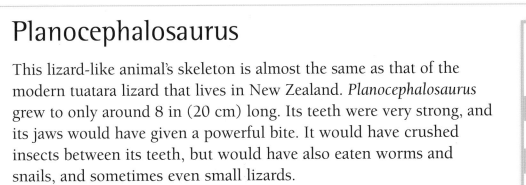

Pleurosaurus

Ju–Cr	Late Jurassic to Early Cretaceous
Size: 2 ft/60 cm long	
Order: Sphenodontida	
Family: Pleurosauridae	
Range: Europe: Germany	
Pronunciation: PLOO-roh-SAW-rus	

Pleurosaurus

Pleurosaurus was a member of the pleurosaur family. The pleurosaurs evolved on land, but returned to the water during the Early Jurassic period. Pleurosaurs had very long bodies. Some of the creatures had up to 57 vertebrae (bones that make up the spine). Snakelike movements of its long body and tail pushed *Pleurosaurus* quickly through the water. Its nostrils were set far back on its snout, close to the eyes. Its legs were quite short and were not used for swimming.

41

Snakes and Lizards

The most successful reptiles today are lizards and snakes. There are some 6,000 species of these reptiles—including walkers, gliders, crawlers, swimmers, climbers, and burrowers. They live in every part of the world except Antarctica. They are descended from an ancient group of diapsid reptiles that dates back over 250 million years. Lizards are a much older group of animals than snakes. The earliest known lizard-like reptiles were small insect-eaters that lived in southern Africa around 250 million years ago. The oldest known snake was from North Africa and is over 100 million years old.

Pachyrhachis

The reptile *Pachyrhachis* had the long body of a snake and the large head of a lizard. It grew to a total length of 3 ft 3 in (1 m). *Pachyrhachis* was a water-dwelling creature. It swam by waving its body from side to side, rather like a snake does to move across land.

Cr	Early Cretaceous
Size:	3 ft 3 in/1 m long
Order:	Squamata
Family:	Pachyrhachidae
Range:	Asia: Israel
Pronunciation:	PAK-ee-RAK-iss

Kuehneosaurus

Kuehneosaurus

This gliding diapsid was once classed as a true lizard, but it is probably more primitive. Its "wings" were made from long ribs that were covered in skin. They spanned more than 1 ft (30 cm). By stretching out its wings and leaping from a tree, *Kuehneosaurus* could glide for long distances. It was a useful technique for escaping from dangerous predators.

Tr	Late Triassic
Size:	26 in/65 cm long
Order:	Unknown
Family:	Kuehneosauridae
Range:	Europe: England
Pronunciation:	CUNE-ee-oh-SAW-rus

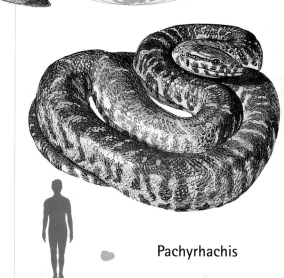

Pachyrhachis

Megalania

Megalania is similar to the modern Komodo dragon lizard, which lives on the islands of Indonesia. *Megalania* hunted on the plains of Australia fewer than 2 million years ago, attacking large animals such as kangaroos that were grazing there. It would have torn off chunks of flesh with its powerful jaws and long, sharp teeth.

Ple Pleistocene	
Size: 26 ft/8 m long	
Order: Squamata	
Family: Varanidae	
Range: Australia: Queensland	
Pronunciation: MEG-ah-LAN-ee-ah	

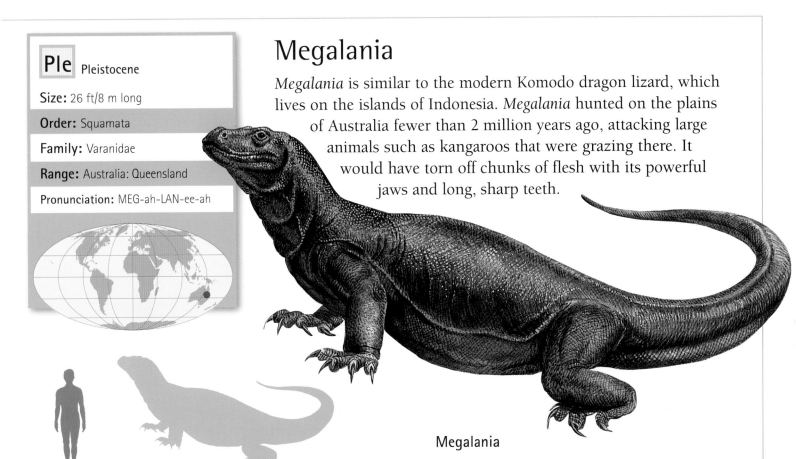

Megalania

Platecarpus

Platecarpus swam in the seas some 75 million years ago. Its tail was as long as its body, and was probably flattened —which made it better for swimming. Snakelike movements of its body would have pushed it through the water. Its short legs and webbed feet were used to steer. This lizard would have eaten fish and soft-bodied creatures, snapping them up in its long, pointed jaws, which were full of sharp teeth.

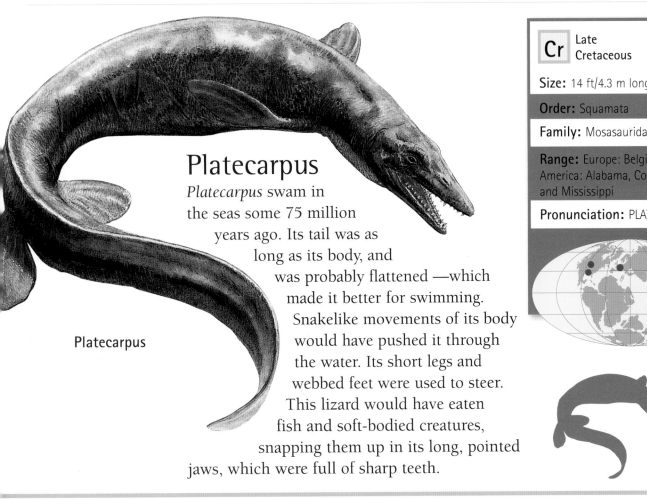

Platecarpus

Cr Late Cretaceous	
Size: 14 ft/4.3 m long	
Order: Squamata	
Family: Mosasauridae	
Range: Europe: Belgium; North America: Alabama, Colorado, Kansas, and Mississippi	
Pronunciation: PLAT-ee-KAR-pus	

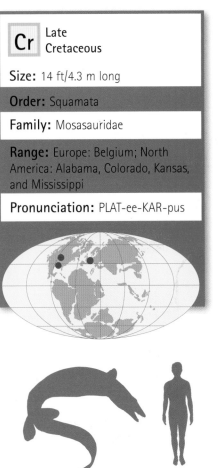

Life in Triassic North America

During the Triassic period, life on Earth was dominated by reptiles. Marine reptiles, such as ichthyosaurs and nothosaurs, swam in the seas, and other reptiles, such as crocodiles and lizards, lived on land. Toward the end of the Triassic period, the ruling reptiles, the first dinosaurs, appeared and spread across the Earth.

The Triassic period lasted for over 40 million years, from 251 to 200 million years ago. At the beginning of the period, the continents were all joined in one great landmass, known as Pangaea. This meant that the animals and plants of the time could easily spread across the world. The climate was warm, and there were no polar ice caps. By the end of the period, however, Pangaea was beginning to break up. The weather had also become cooler and wetter. This new environment brought about big changes in the vertebrates (animals with backbones). Reptiles flourished and, at the end of Triassic times, the first dinosaurs arrived on Earth.

Early Prosauropod: Massospondylus

Massospondylus, which means "massive vertebra," was named for the huge bones that make up its spine. The dinosaur was first discovered in South Africa in 1854 by the English paleontologist Richard Owen. In the 1980s, further fossils were discovered in Arizona, U.S.A.

Massospondylus had a tiny head perched on a long and flexible neck. Its five-fingered hands were massive and very wide. They could have been used for walking or for holding food. Each "thumb" had a large, curved claw.

Polished stones have been found in the stomachs of some *Massospondylus* skeletons. The dinosaur would have swallowed stones with rough edges to help grind up the tough plants that it ate. Many modern birds eat stones for just the same reason. Since *Massospondylus* probably spent most of its time eating, the surface of these stones would have been polished smooth in a short time.

Once the rough surfaces of the stones were worn down, they were no of further use. *Massospondylus* would then vomit them up and swallow new, rough stones.

44

Carnivorous Ceratosaur: Coelophysis

Bones of *Coelophysis* were found in 1947 at Ghost Ranch in New Mexico. Several skeletons of different sizes were found together. There were very young dinosaurs and also adults, ranging in length from 3 to 10 ft (1 to 3 m). They probably lived together as a group, and must have all died at the same time.

This dinosaur was built for speed and would have been a terrifying hunter. Its slender body probably weighed less than 50 lb (23 kg). The neck, tail, and legs were long and slim, and the tail made up about half the body length. The long, narrow head was armed with many sharp teeth, each with a knifelike edge. Coelophysis had feet like those of a bird: each foot had three walking toes with sharp claws. There were four fingers on each hand, though only three were strong enough to grasp prey.

Coelophysis probably lived in the forests, hunting in packs close to streams and lakes. Its prey would have included small, shrewlike mammals.

Two of the adult skeletons found in New Mexico contained the bones of tiny *Coelophysis* inside their bodies. At first, paleontologists thought that this meant *Coelophysis* gave birth to live young, rather than laying eggs like most other reptiles. But the hip bones were too narrow—*Coelophyisis* wouldn't have been able to give birth. So it seems that this dinosaur sometimes ate its own species.

Below: In Triassic North America, a great deal of the land was desert. Most plants grew around lakes or around pools that formed after heavy rainfall. This scene shows different animals by a drying lake. The animals include *Coelophysis*, a fast-moving hunter dinosaur; *Metoposaurus*, a giant amphibian; and *Trilophosaurus*, a plant-eating reptile. In the background is *Massospondylus*, one of the first long-necked dinosaurs.

Massospondylus

Coelophysis

Trilophosaurus

Metoposaurus

Turtles, Tortoises, and Terrapins

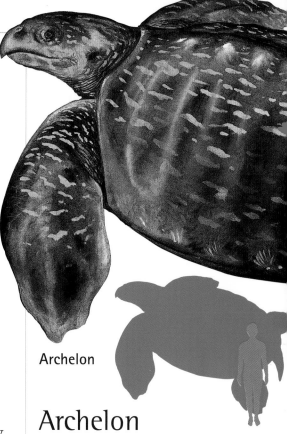

Today's turtles, tortoises, and terrapins are the only survivors of an ancient group of reptiles called the testudins or chelonians. They are different from all other reptiles—their bodies are inside a shell, except for the head, tail, and legs. Many testudins can pull their heads and legs into the shell for more protection. Today's turtles and tortoises have hardly changed in over 200 million years.

Archelon

Archelon

This giant sea turtle had a shell of thick, rubbery skin. Its limbs were like massive paddles to push the animal through the water. Like the modern leatherback turtle, *Archelon* probably ate jellyfish as its main food. The soft jellyfish were easily cut even by the turtle's weak jaws and toothless beak.

Ple Pleistocene
Size: 8 ft/2.5 m long
Order: Testudines
Family: Testudinidae
Range: Asia: India
Pronunciation: TEST-oo-doh AT-las

Testudo atlas

Testudo atlas was the largest tortoise ever to walk the Earth. Sometimes it is called *Colossochelys*, which means "colossal shell." This mighty creature weighed about 4.5 U.S. tons (4 tonnes). Its huge legs stretched out at the sides of its body to hold up its massive shell, which protected it against predator attacks.

Cr Late Cretaceous
Size: 12 ft/3.7 m long
Order: Testudines
Family: Protostegidae
Range: North America: Kansas and South Dakota
Pronunciation: ar-KEE-lon

Testudo atlas

Meiolania

Meiolania was a large, well-protected tortoise. Its head had large spikes, two of which stuck out on either side. These spikes made the animal's head 2 ft (60 cm) wide. The spikes meant that *Meiolania* probably could not pull its head back into its shell in times of danger. However, the shell protected its back, and its tail had rings of bony armor. The tail also ended in a spiked club, which could have been used to hit attackers.

Cr	Late Cretaceous
Size: 8 ft/2.5 m long	
Order: Testudines	
Family: Meiolaniidae	
Range: Australia: Queensland, New Caledonia, and Lord Howe Island	
Pronunciation: MY-oh-LAN-ee-ah	

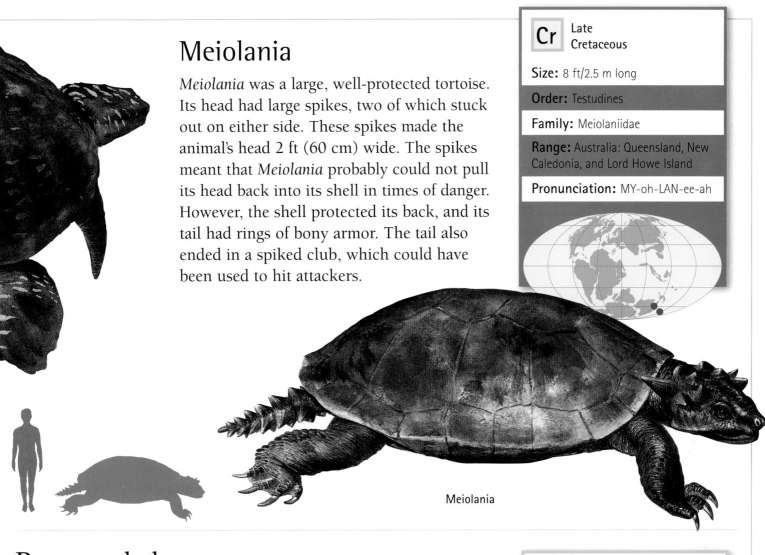

Meiolania

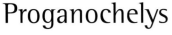

Proganochelys

Proganochelys was very similar to a modern land-living tortoise, but it could not pull its head or legs into its shell. The body of this ancient tortoise was short and wide. Only 10 long bones made up its backbone. *Proganochelys*' short neck and head were armed with bony knobs. The creature had a broad, domed shell (known as a carapace) covering its back, and flat plates protected it underneath. About 60 plates made up the shell.

Tr	Late Triassic
Size: 3 ft 3 in/1 m long	
Order: Testudines	
Family: Proganochelidae	
Range: Europe: Germany	
Pronunciation: PRO-gan-oh-KEEL-is	

Proganochelys

47

Placodonts

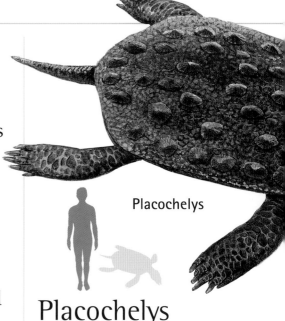

Placochelys

uring the Mesozoic Era (251–65 million years ago), several groups of reptiles returned to the sea. There their bodies had to adapt to living in the water. Placodonts lived in shallow waters or on the shore. They did not go out into very deep waters, but swam along the coast, where they could find plenty of shellfish to eat. Their broad teeth would grind the shellfish up for swallowing. Many placodonts had hard shells like those of modern turtles. These protected their soft bodies from attack by predators. Placodonts lived on Earth for about 35 million years.

Placochelys

This small reptile was well-adapted to life in the seas. It had a turtle-like body and tough knobby plates covered the creature's back. These plates made a kind of protective body armor. *Placochelys'* tail was short, and its limbs were like long paddles for swimming.

Placodus

The skull of *Placodus* shows that its teeth were good for eating a diet of shellfish. Rows of blunt teeth at the front of the jaws were used to pull shellfish off the rocks. The back teeth were broad and flat, for crushing the shells. Even the roof of the mouth was covered with large, crushing teeth. The teeth were powered by massive jaw muscles. Some modern sharks that eat hard-shelled animals have the same kind of teeth.

Tr	Early to Middle Triassic

Size: 6 ft 6 in/2 m long

Order: Placodontia

Family: Placodontidae

Range: Europe: Alps

Pronunciation: PLAK-oh-dus

Placodus

Tr	Middle to Late Triassic

Size: 3 ft/90 cm long

Order: Placodontia

Family: Cyamodontidae

Range: Europe: Germany

Pronunciation: PLAK-oh-CHEL-is

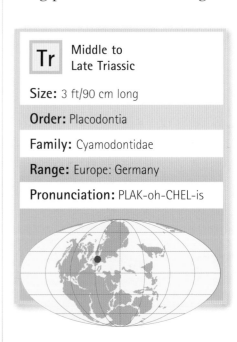

Henodus

The body of *Henodus* was as wide as it was long. This is the same shape as that of a modern turtle. Its back and belly were covered with bony plates. These made a defensive shell to protect it from attack by other marine reptiles, such as the ichthyosaurs. *Henodus*' head was very square and boxlike and there were no teeth in its jaws. Instead, it probably had a horny beak, similar to that of a modern turtle, which could be used to both pull shellfish off the rocks and crush them up for eating.

Size: 3 ft 3 in/1 m long

Order: Placodontia

Family: Henodontidae

Range: Europe: Germany

Pronunciation: HEN-oh-dus

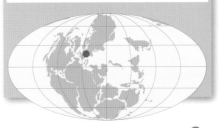

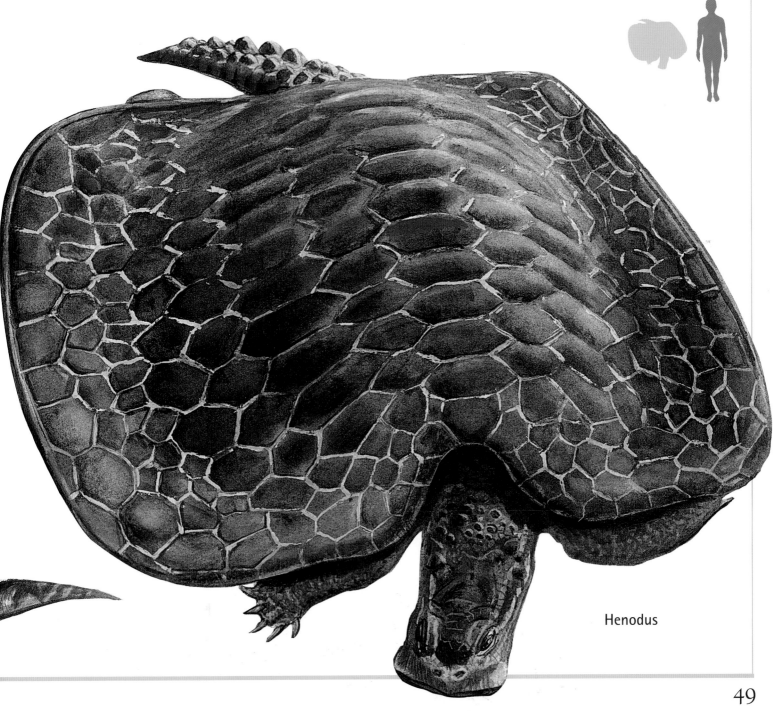

Henodus

49

Nothosaurs

Nothosaurs were fish-eating marine reptiles. Their necks, bodies, and tails were long, their feet were webbed, and they had many sharp teeth in their jaws. The long necks helped the nothosaurs catch their prey, as they could reach out and snap up passing fish. Their front legs were much stronger than their back legs, which suggests that the front legs were used more for swimming. Nothosaurs lived and died out during the Triassic period. Some paleontologists believe that they may have been a halfway stage between the land-living reptiles and the sea-living plesiosaurs.

Tr	Middle Triassic
Size: 2 ft/60 cm long	
Order: Nothosauria	
Family: Nothosauridae	
Range: Europe: Germany, Italy, Spain, and Switzerland	
Pronunciation: LAH-ree-oh-SAW-rus	

Lariosaurus

Nothosaurus

This creature probably lived as modern seals do, fishing at sea and resting on land. Its feet had five long, webbed toes. The body, neck, and tail were long and flexible. It probably had a fin on its back to help with steering underwater. The jaws of *Nothosaurus* were long and slim, with sharp, interlocking teeth.

Lariosaurus

Lariosaurus was one of the smaller nothosaurs. It was not the smallest, however—some of them were only 8 in (20 cm) long. It had a short neck and short toes. This reptile probably spent much of its time walking about on the seashore or paddling around in shallow waters. It fed on small fish and shrimp.

Tr	Early to Late Triassic
Size: 10 ft/3 m long	
Order: Nothosauria	
Family: Nothosauridae	
Range: Asia: China and Israel; Russia; Europe: Germany, Netherlands, and Switzerland; North Africa	
Pronunciation: NOTH-oh-SAW-rus	

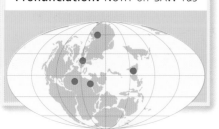

Nothosaurus

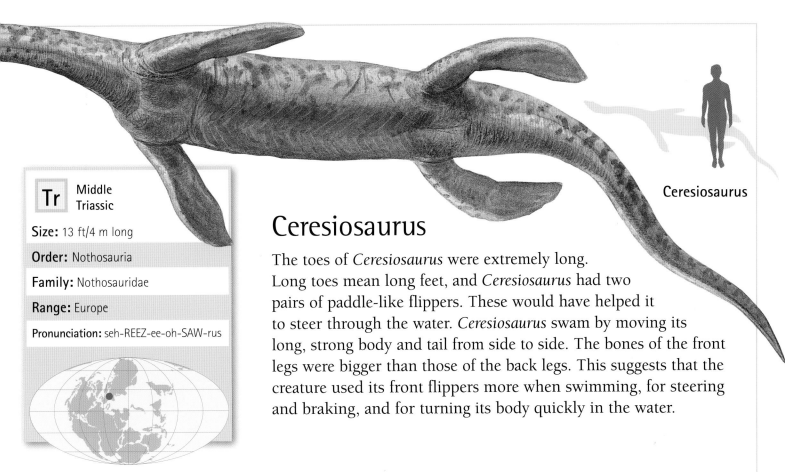

Ceresiosaurus

Tr	Middle Triassic

Size: 13 ft/4 m long

Order: Nothosauria

Family: Nothosauridae

Range: Europe

Pronunciation: seh-REEZ-ee-oh-SAW-rus

Ceresiosaurus

The toes of *Ceresiosaurus* were extremely long. Long toes mean long feet, and *Ceresiosaurus* had two pairs of paddle-like flippers. These would have helped it to steer through the water. *Ceresiosaurus* swam by moving its long, strong body and tail from side to side. The bones of the front legs were bigger than those of the back legs. This suggests that the creature used its front flippers more when swimming, for steering and braking, and for turning its body quickly in the water.

Pistosaurus

Pistosaurus had features of both the nothosaur and the plesiosaur groups. Its skull was like that of a plesiosaur, but the roof of its mouth was like that of a nothosaur. Although it had a body like a nothosaur, it swam by pushing itself through the water with paddle-like limbs like a pleisosaur. Nothosaurs used the movement of their bodies to swim. *Pistosaurus* had a mouthful of sharp, pointed teeth. It was a fish-eater and would have snapped up prey with its powerful jaws.

Tr	Middle Triassic

Size: 10 ft/3 m long

Order: Nothosauria

Family: Pistosauridae

Range: Europe: France and Germany

Pronunciation: PIS-toe-SAW-rus

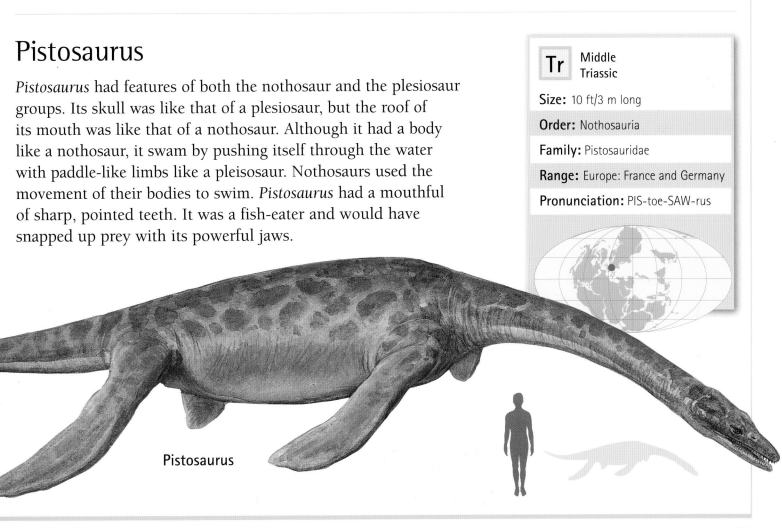

Pistosaurus

Plesiosaurs

Plesiosaurs were huge, reaching lengths of up to 46 ft (14 m). To adapt to life in the sea, their limbs had evolved into long, narrow flippers, ideal for swimming. At one time, paleontologists believed that the plesiosaurs used their flippers like enormous oars, "rowing" themselves through the water. However, today experts think they moved their flippers like the wings of a bird, and that plesiosaurs in fact "flew" through the water. Their "wings" were like those of modern penguins or turtles.

Ju	Late Jurassic
Size: 20 ft/6 m long	
Order: Plesiosauria	
Family: Elasmosauridae	
Range: Europe: England and France	
Pronunciation: mu-RI-no-SAW-rus	

Muraenosaurus

Cryptoclidus

Cryptoclidus had a long neck and snout, and long, flexible flippers. It also had a large number of very sharply-pointed, curved teeth. These teeth locked together when the mouth was closed, acting like a cage to trap small fish or shrimp.

Muraenosaurus

Muraenosaurus belonged to a group of creatures called elasmosaurs. Elasmosaurs had the longest necks of all plesiosaurs. *Muraenosaurus'* neck was as long as its body and tail put together. Its head was tiny and its body was short and stiff.

Ju	Late Jurassic
Size: 13 ft/4 m long	
Order: Plesiosauria	
Family: Cryptoclididae	
Range: Europe: England	
Pronunciation: KRIP-toe-KLIDE-us	

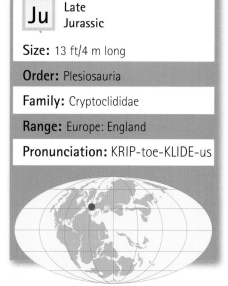

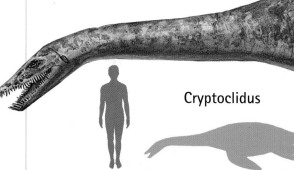

Cryptoclidus

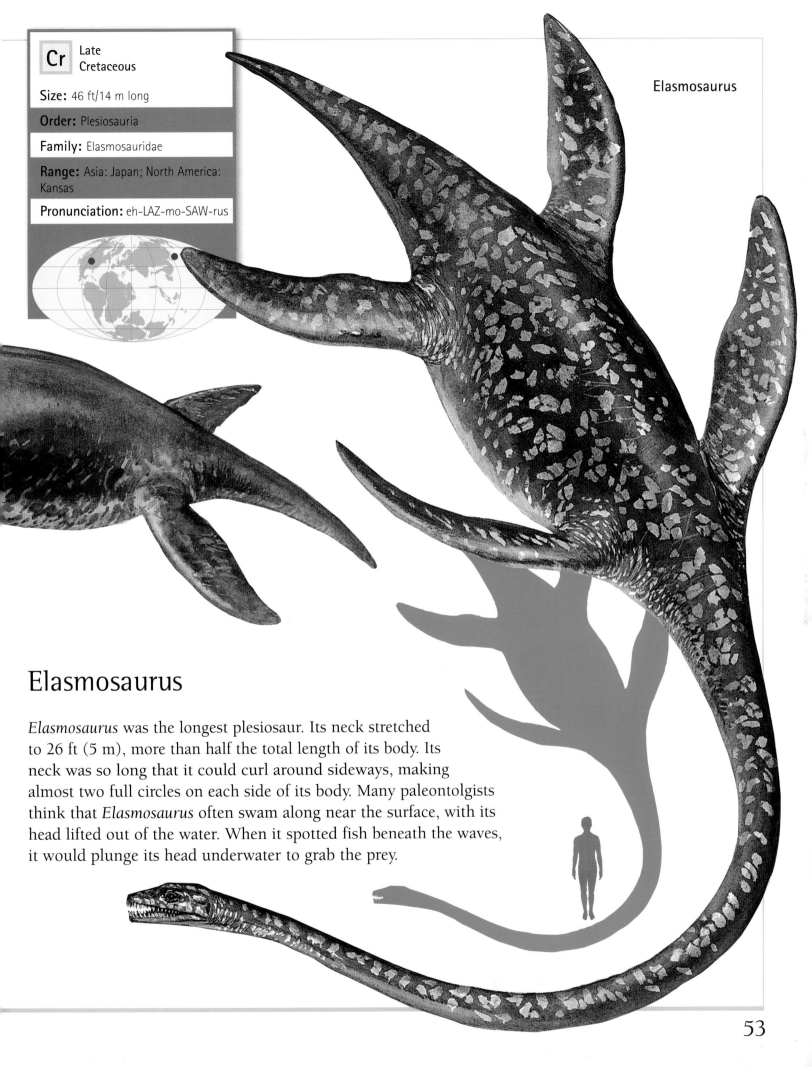

Cr Late Cretaceous

Size: 46 ft/14 m long

Order: Plesiosauria

Family: Elasmosauridae

Range: Asia: Japan; North America: Kansas

Pronunciation: eh-LAZ-mo-SAW-rus

Elasmosaurus

Elasmosaurus was the longest plesiosaur. Its neck stretched to 26 ft (5 m), more than half the total length of its body. Its neck was so long that it could curl around sideways, making almost two full circles on each side of its body. Many paleontolgists think that *Elasmosaurus* often swam along near the surface, with its head lifted out of the water. When it spotted fish beneath the waves, it would plunge its head underwater to grab the prey.

Life in Jurassic Seas

Many reptiles, including plesiosaurs and ichthyosaurs, lived in the Jurassic seas. The ichthyosaurs grew up to 50 ft (15 m) long. They were good at deep diving, with large eyes for hunting in dark waters. Plesiosaurs ranged in size from 6 to 45 ft (2 to 14 m) and were very well adapted for swimming, with four large, paddle-shaped limbs.

Ichthyosaurs had mouths full of small, sharp, cone-shaped teeth. These were ideal for snatching and holding fish before swallowing them whole. With their slim bodies, many ichthyosaurs looked like dolphins. They could also swim at high speeds like dolphins when hunting small, fast-swimming fish. Plesiosaurs had small skulls and long snouts. They had to come to the surface to breathe. Their jaws were full of crocodile-like teeth, helpful for holding slippery fish. There was a group of short-necked plesiosaurs, called pliosaurs. The pliosaurs had large skulls and they swam faster than the long-necked plesiosaurs.

Marine Reptile: Plesiosaurus

Plesiosaurs changed little during the 135 million years that they were on the Earth. The earliest known member of the group was called *Plesiosaurus*. This creature had all the features that later plesiosaurs would have, including a long neck, a small skull packed with sharp teeth, powerful flippers, and a slim body.

A plesiosaur was built for twisting and turning easily underwater, rather than for swimming at high speed. When hunting small fish it would need to move its body around quickly to snap up prey. A forward stroke by the flippers on one side of the body, and a backward stroke by the flippers on the other side, would have turned the animal's short body almost on the spot. Its long neck could then dart out swiftly to catch fast-swimming prey.

Ammonite

Plesiosaurus

Rhomaleosaurus

Marine Reptile: Ichthyosaurus

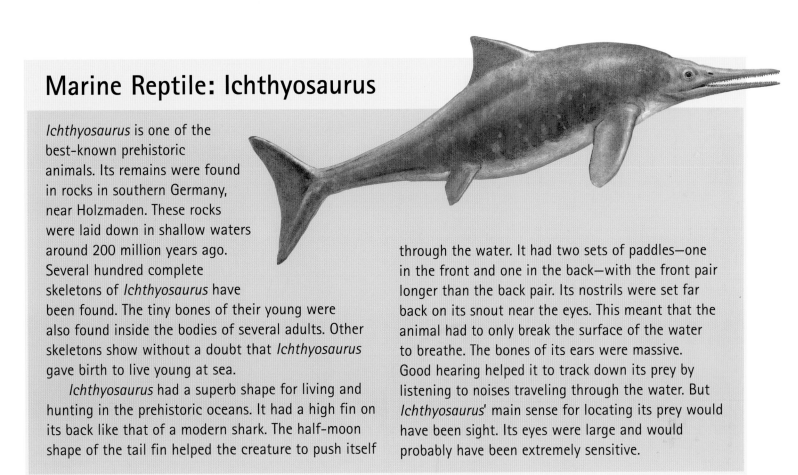

Ichthyosaurus is one of the best-known prehistoric animals. Its remains were found in rocks in southern Germany, near Holzmaden. These rocks were laid down in shallow waters around 200 million years ago. Several hundred complete skeletons of *Ichthyosaurus* have been found. The tiny bones of their young were also found inside the bodies of several adults. Other skeletons show without a doubt that *Ichthyosaurus* gave birth to live young at sea.

Ichthyosaurus had a superb shape for living and hunting in the prehistoric oceans. It had a high fin on its back like that of a modern shark. The half-moon shape of the tail fin helped the creature to push itself through the water. It had two sets of paddles—one in the front and one in the back—with the front pair longer than the back pair. Its nostrils were set far back on its snout near the eyes. This meant that the animal had to only break the surface of the water to breathe. The bones of its ears were massive. Good hearing helped it to track down its prey by listening to noises traveling through the water. But *Ichthyosaurus*' main sense for locating its prey would have been sight. Its eyes were large and would probably have been extremely sensitive.

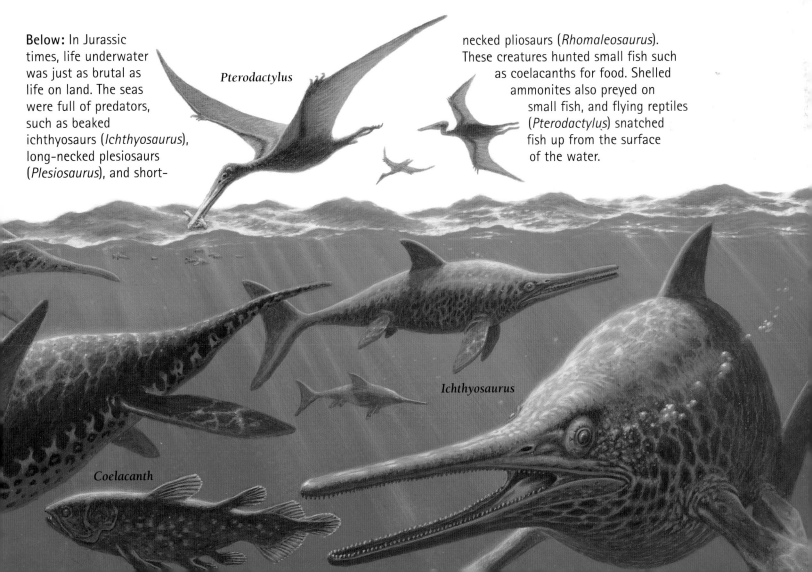

Below: In Jurassic times, life underwater was just as brutal as life on land. The seas were full of predators, such as beaked ichthyosaurs (*Ichthyosaurus*), long-necked plesiosaurs (*Plesiosaurus*), and short-necked pliosaurs (*Rhomaleosaurus*). These creatures hunted small fish such as coelacanths for food. Shelled ammonites also preyed on small fish, and flying reptiles (*Pterodactylus*) snatched fish up from the surface of the water.

Pterodactylus

Ichthyosaurus

Coelacanth

Pliosaurs

Pliosaurs first appeared around 200 million years ago in the Early Jurassic period. They became the tigers of the seas, chasing and killing large sea creatures such as sharks, ichthyosaurs, and even their relatives, the plesiosaurs. They had large heads with very strong teeth and jaws, powered by huge jaw muscles. Some pliosaurs had heads almost 10 ft (3 m) long.

Ju	Late Jurassic
Size: 10 ft/3 m long	
Order: Plesiosauria	
Family: Pliosauroidea	
Range: Russia; Europe: England	
Pronunciation: pel-oh-nee-OOST-ees	

Peloneustes

Macroplata

Macroplata, an early pliosaur, had a crocodile-like skull. Its long neck was twice the length of its head. The pliosaur's front and back limbs were strong, powerful paddles. Unlike the plesiosaurs, however, the back limbs, rather than the front, became the biggest in pliosaurs. This suggests they used the back limbs more when swimming.

Ju	Early Jurassic
Size: 15 ft/4.5 m long	
Order: Plesiosauria	
Family: Pliosauroidea	
Range: Europe: England	
Pronunciation: MAC-roh-PLAY-tu	

Macroplata

Peloneustes

Peloneustes had a larger head but a shorter neck than *Macroplata* (left). Its head and neck were almost the same length. *Peloneustes'* shape helped it to swim quickly after its fast-moving prey. The teeth were not as many and were less sharp than those of the fish-eating plesiosaurs. They were better for catching soft squid and crushing the hard shells of ammonites. When hunting, it used its long head, as well as its neck, to reach prey.

Kronosaurus

The Australian *Kronosaurus* is the largest known pliosaur. It lived in warm, shallow seas and would have been an agile swimmer. Its skull was massively long, measuring 9 ft (2.7 m). Its jaws were even longer and more powerful than those of the greatest meat-eating dinosaur—*Tyrannosaurus*.

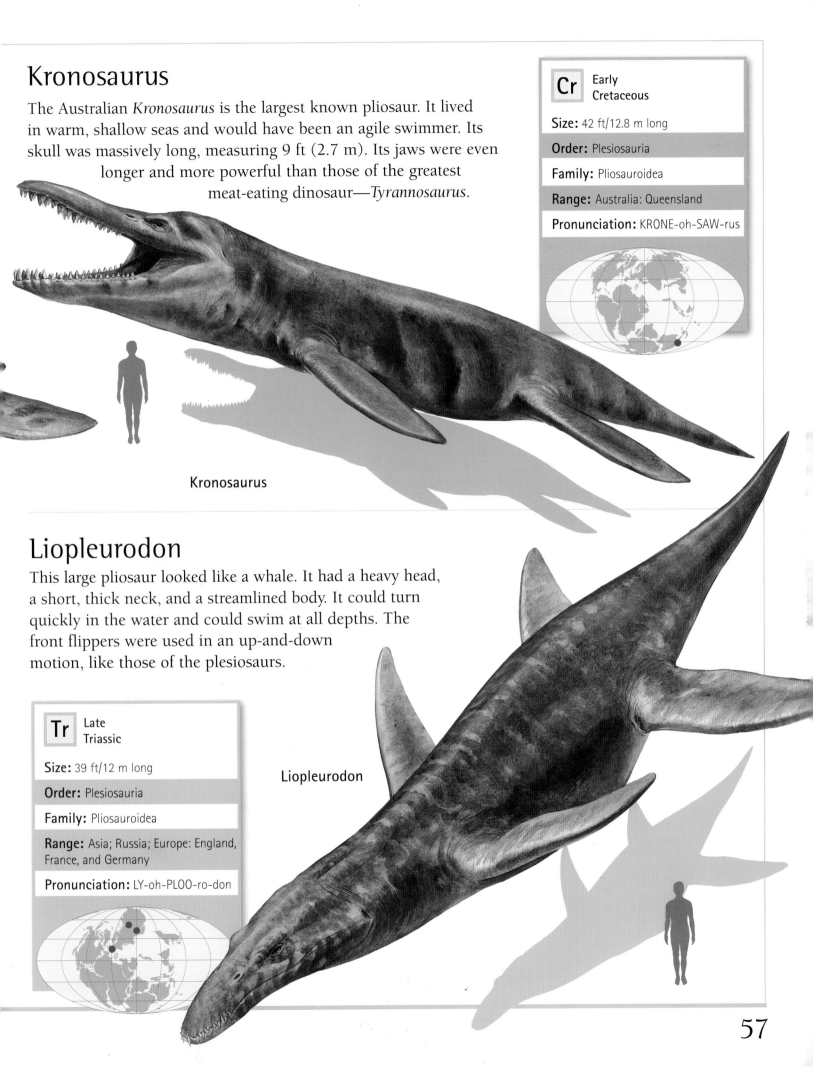

Cr	Early Cretaceous
Size: 42 ft/12.8 m long	
Order: Plesiosauria	
Family: Pliosauroidea	
Range: Australia: Queensland	
Pronunciation: KRONE-oh-SAW-rus	

Kronosaurus

Liopleurodon

This large pliosaur looked like a whale. It had a heavy head, a short, thick neck, and a streamlined body. It could turn quickly in the water and could swim at all depths. The front flippers were used in an up-and-down motion, like those of the plesiosaurs.

Tr	Late Triassic
Size: 39 ft/12 m long	
Order: Plesiosauria	
Family: Pliosauroidea	
Range: Asia; Russia; Europe: England, France, and Germany	
Pronunciation: LY-oh-PLOO-ro-don	

Liopleurodon

57

Ichthyosaurs

The name ichthyosaur means "fish lizard." This describes ichthyosaurs well, since although they ate fish and were shaped like fish, they were in fact air-breathing reptiles. Their bodies were shaped like those of modern mackerel or tuna. Ichthyosaurs were agile creatures, and could swim at speeds of over 25 mph (40 km/h). Unlike the plesiosaurs, ichthyosaurs did not rely on their paddle-like flippers for swimming. Instead, they had fishlike tails. These creatures thrashed their tails from side to side to push themselves quickly through the water, just like modern sharks.

Tr	Middle Triassic
Size: 3 ft 3 in/1 m long	
Order: Ichthyosauria	
Family: Mixosauridae	
Range: Asia: China and Timor, Indonesia; Europe: Alps; North America: Alaska, Canadian Arctic, and Nevada; Spitsbergen	
Pronunciation: MIX-oh-SAW-rus	

Mixosaurus

Mixosaurus had a fishlike body with a fin on its back. It probably also had the beginnings of a fin on the top of its tail. Its limbs were like short paddles, and the front pair was longer than the back pair. Each paddle had five long, bony toes. Its jaws were also long and narrow, and were equipped with sharp teeth. *Mixosaurus'* teeth were well adapted for catching and eating fish.

Shonisaurus

Shonisaurus is the largest known ichthyosaur. It had a fishlike shape and its enormous length was divided into three equal parts—the head and neck, the body, and the tail. *Shonisaurus* had very long jaws and only had teeth at the front of its mouth. Its limbs looked like extra-long, narrow paddles and were, unusually, all the same size. The front pair of limbs in most ichthyosaurs was usually longer than the back pair.

Tr	Late Triassic
Size: 43 ft/15 m long	
Order: Ichthyosauria	
Family: Shastasauridae	
Range: North America: Nevada	
Pronunciation: SHOWN-ih-SAW-rus	

Mixosaurus

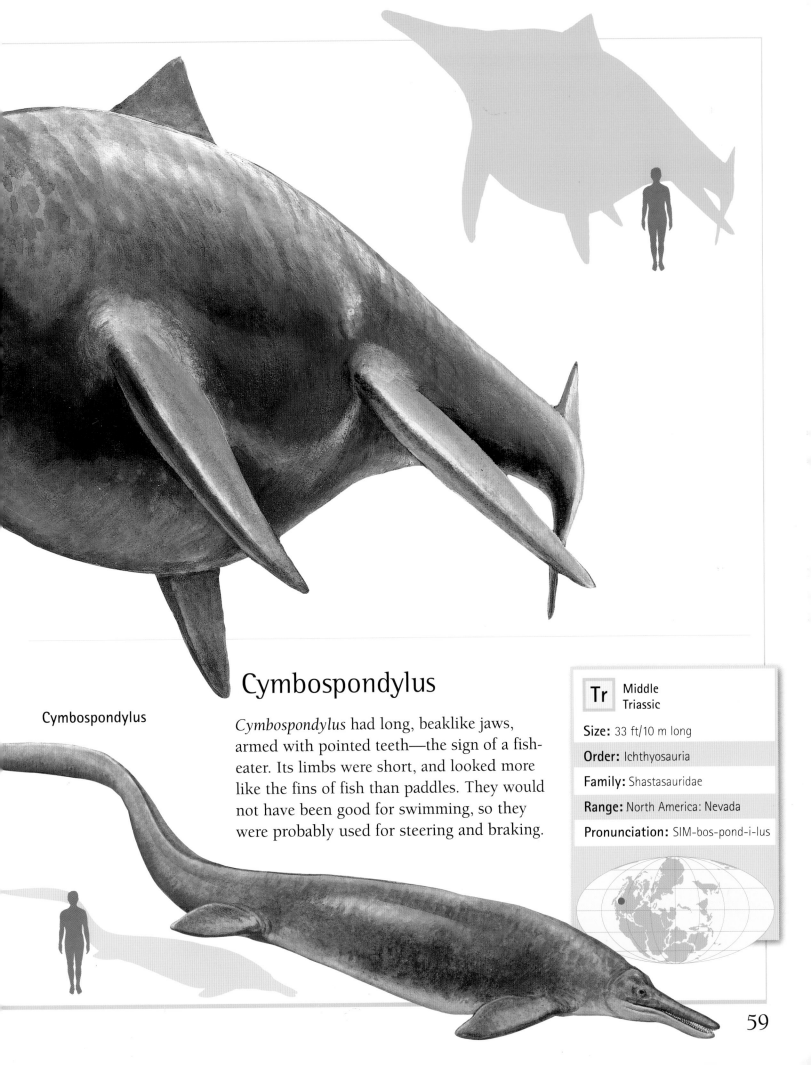

Cymbospondylus

Cymbospondylus

Cymbospondylus had long, beaklike jaws, armed with pointed teeth—the sign of a fish-eater. Its limbs were short, and looked more like the fins of fish than paddles. They would not have been good for swimming, so they were probably used for steering and braking.

Tr Middle Triassic

Size: 33 ft/10 m long

Order: Ichthyosauria

Family: Shastasauridae

Range: North America: Nevada

Pronunciation: SIM-bos-pond-i-lus

Ju	Late Jurassic

Size: 11 ft 6 in/3.5 m long

Order: Ichthyosauria

Family: Ichthyosauridae

Range: Europe: England and France; North America: western USA and Canadian Arctic; South America: Argentina

Pronunciation: OFF-thal-moh-SAW-rus

Stenopterygius

During the Jurassic period, there were two types of ichthyosaur. The shape of the paddle-like limbs of each type were different. *Ichthyosaurus* (see p.55) and animals like it had short, broad paddles that had up to nine toes. *Stenopterygius* had narrower paddles made up of just five toes.

Ju	Early to Middle Jurassic

Size: 10 ft/3 m long

Order: Ichthyosauria

Family: Stenopterygiidae

Range: Europe: England and Germany

Pronunciation: STEN-op-ter-IJ-ius

Opthalmosaurus

Ophthalmosaurus' front flippers were much stronger than its back ones, which suggests the front flippers were used more when steering. *Ophthalmosaurus'* most amazing feature was its huge eyes. These were about 4 in (10 cm) across. The super-large eyes might mean that it could see well in the dark of the ocean. It probably fed on squid.

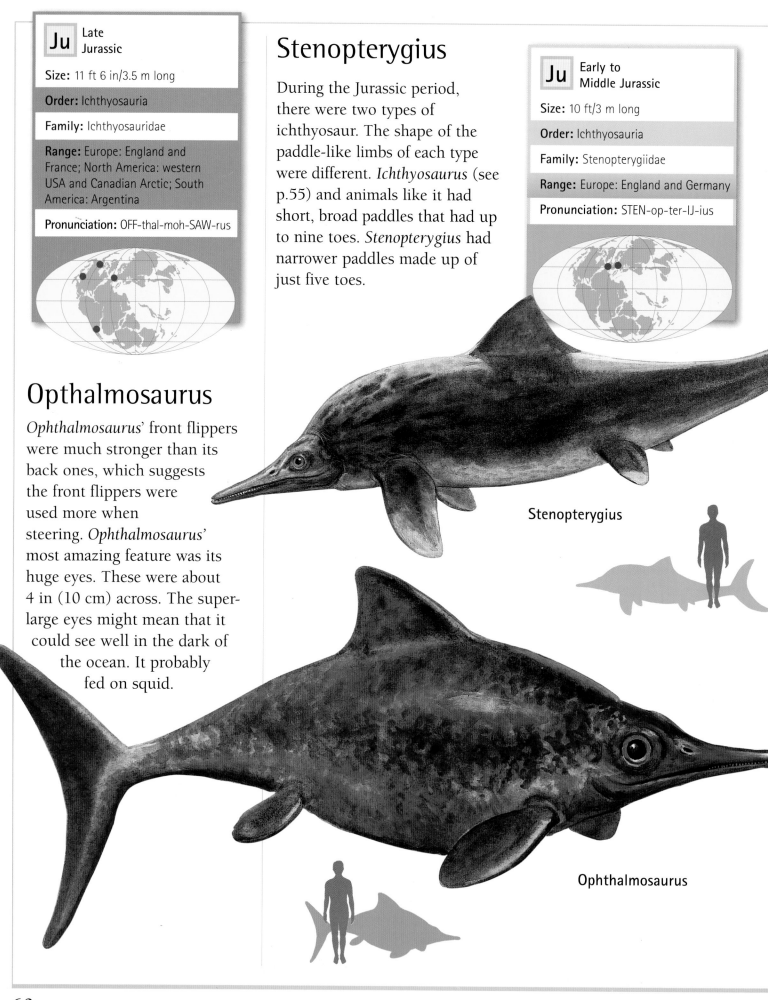

Stenopterygius

Ophthalmosaurus

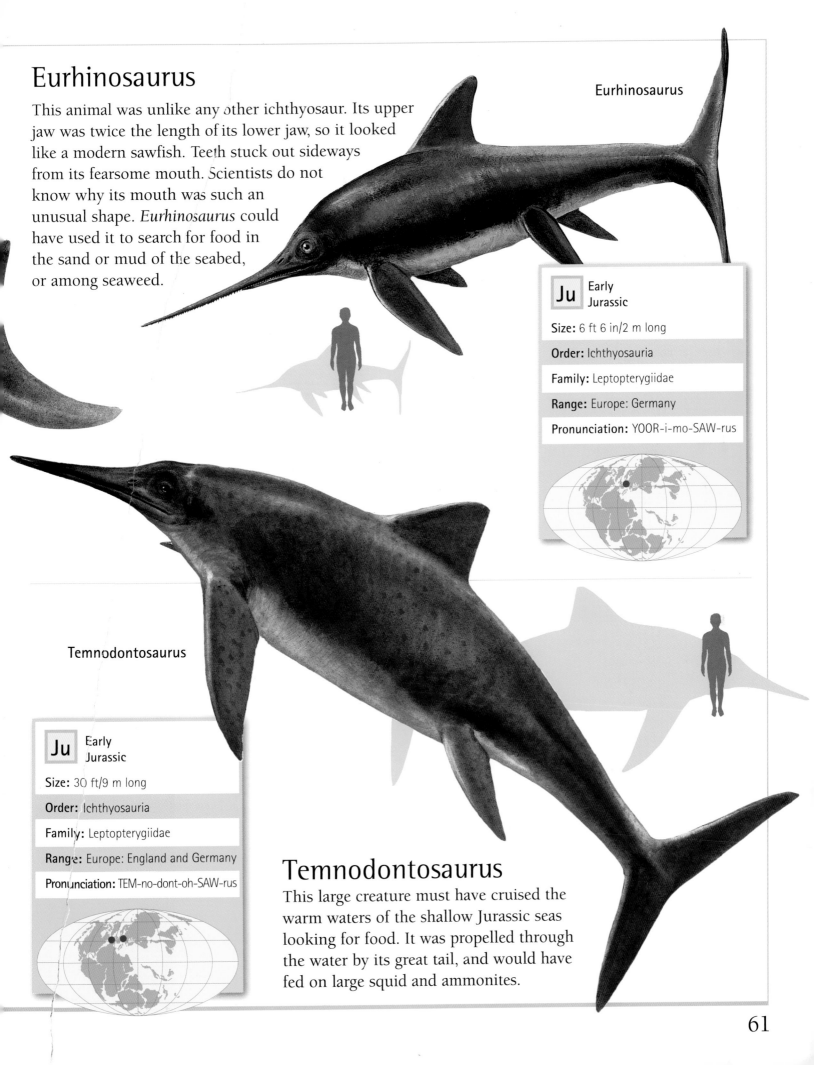

Eurhinosaurus

This animal was unlike any other ichthyosaur. Its upper jaw was twice the length of its lower jaw, so it looked like a modern sawfish. Teeth stuck out sideways from its fearsome mouth. Scientists do not know why its mouth was such an unusual shape. *Eurhinosaurus* could have used it to search for food in the sand or mud of the seabed, or among seaweed.

Eurhinosaurus

Ju	Early Jurassic
Size: 6 ft 6 in/2 m long	
Order: Ichthyosauria	
Family: Leptopterygiidae	
Range: Europe: Germany	
Pronunciation: YOOR-i-mo-SAW-rus	

Temnodontosaurus

Ju	Early Jurassic
Size: 30 ft/9 m long	
Order: Ichthyosauria	
Family: Leptopterygiidae	
Range: Europe: England and Germany	
Pronunciation: TEM-no-dont-oh-SAW-rus	

Temnodontosaurus

This large creature must have cruised the warm waters of the shallow Jurassic seas looking for food. It was propelled through the water by its great tail, and would have fed on large squid and ammonites.

The Beast of Maastricht

In 1786 an amazing discovery was made. Some huge jaw bones were found in a quarry near Maastricht in Holland. Years later, scientists realized that the bones belonged to a type of giant water-dwelling lizard called a mosasaur. The creature lived about 70 million years ago, when water covered the area. At that time, the sea was home to many different marine animals. In 1998, scientists working in the same quarry made another important find—a nearly complete skeleton of a mosasaur. This skeleton was about 46 ft (14 m) long. The remains of other mosasaurs have also been found in other parts of Europe, North America, Africa, Australia, and New Zealand.

Mosasaurs

These giant sea-dwelling lizards became extinct around 65 million years ago. There may have been as many as 70 species of mosasaurs. The smallest of these was called *Carinodens*. It was about 10 ft (3 m) long and may have lived on the sea floor, where is ate mollusks and sea urchins. The largest was *Mosasaurus hoffmani*, which grew to 50 ft (15 m) long. Mosasaurs were fast swimmers. They pushed themselves through the water by moving their huge tails from side to side. The paddle-like flippers were used to help steer the body.

Mosasaurus hoffmani

The tail moved from side to side for swimming power

Ocean Predator

Mosasaurus hoffmani had a powerful skull and long jaws. The jaws were lined with strong teeth able to bite and crush prey. It probably snapped up fish and squid, but may also have attacked ammonites—these were like squid but with hard shells. Many ammonite shells have been found showing marks made by teeth shaped like those of mosasaurs. Some of these shells appear to have been bitten several times in different places as the mosasaur tried to reach the flesh inside.

Huge, powerful jaws

Flippers

Below: This picture shows the discovery of the massive jaw bones of *Mosasaurus hoffmani*. The bones were found in an old chalk mine in Maastricht, Holland, in 1786. The discovery caused enormous excitement among European scientists. Experts couldn't decide what the creature was. A scientist named Pieter Camper thought it was a whale, but later his son realized it was a huge lizard. French paleontologist Baron Georges Cuvier called the creature *Mosasaurus*. This name means "lizard from the River Meuse" (a river that runs through Maastricht).

Early Ruling Reptiles

(see p.38)

Around 250 million years ago, diapsid reptiles (see p.38) divided into two important groups. First, there were the archosauromorphs, which means "ruling reptile forms," or early ruling reptiles. From this group came dinosaurs, crocodiles, and birds. The second group was the lepidosauromorphs, which led to the snakes and lizards. Most archosauromorphs were land-living animals. Their long legs of were held more directly under the body than in other reptiles. This gave them better balance and meant they could move faster. The shape of their feet and ankle joints was also improved. The big toes became more flexible, which helped them to move around on land more easily.

Pe	Late Permian
Size: 6 ft 6 in/2 m long	
Order: Prolacertiformes	
Family: Protorosauridae	
Range: Europe: Germany	
Pronunciation: PROTO-row-SAW-rus	

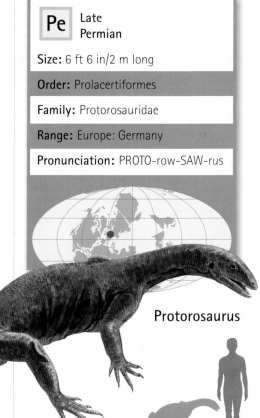

Protorosaurus

Hyperodapedon

Tr	Late Triassic
Size: 4 ft/1.3 m long	
Order: Rhynchosauria	
Family: Rhynchosauridae	
Range: Asia: India; Europe: Scotland	
Pronunciation: HYPER-oh-DAP-e-don	

Hyperodapedon was a heavy, barrel-shaped plant-eater. It had several rows of teeth on its upper jaw, and two single rows on its lower jaw. Its teeth were designed to chop up the toughest of plants. It would have fed on seed ferns, which were found everywhere during the Triassic period. When these plants died out and were replaced by conifers at the end of that period, *Hyperodapedon* died out, too.

Protorosaurus

This lizard-like reptile lived in the deserts of Europe about 250 million years ago. It is the earliest known archosauromorph. *Protorosaurus* would have been a speedy animal. Its long legs were tucked in under its body, allowing it to chase after fast-moving prey. It mainly ate insects. Its neck was made up of seven large and very long bones.

Hyperodapedon

Tr Early Triassic

Size: 6 ft 6 in/2 m long

Order: Archosauria

Family: Proterosuchidae

Range: Asia: China

Pronunciation: KAS-mat-oh-SAW-rus

Chasmatosaurus

Chasmatosaurus

Chasmatosaurus looked rather like a modern crocodile. It also probably behaved in much the same way. Its powerful limbs each had five toes, and each leg stretched out to the side of its body. Although *Chasmatosaurus* could walk on land, it probably spent most of its time in rivers, where it fed on fish using its sharp, curved teeth.

Tanystropheus

Tanystropheus must have been an astonishing sight. Its neck was longer than its body and tail put together. Amazingly, only 10 vertebrae made up the neck—only three more than in *Protorosaurus* (left). Its neck bones were so long that they were thought to be leg bones when they were first discovered. *Tanystropheus'* shape is so bizarre that some paleontologists believe that this creature would have been unable to carry its extremely long neck on land and that it must have lived in water. But *Tanystropheus* does not seem to have the body of a swimming animal. Perhaps it lived on the shoreline, dipping its head into the water after fish or shellfish. It would crush up its food with its peglike teeth.

Tr Middle Triassic

Size: 10 ft/3 m long

Order: Prolacertiformes

Family: Tanystropheidae

Range: Asia: Israel; Europe: Germany and Switzerland

Pronunciation: TAN-ee-STRO-fee-us

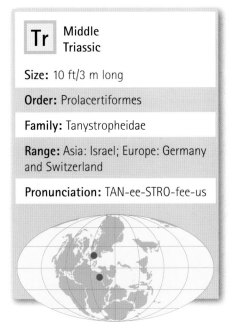

Tanystropheus

65

Erythrosuchus

Erythrosuchus was one of the largest land-living meat-eaters during the Early and Middle Triassic period (about 250–245 million years ago). Some of these creatures were 16 ft (5 m) long. *Erythrosuchus* also had a large head, up to 3 ft 3 in (1 m) long, and powerful jaws filled with sharp, conical teeth. Its legs were held more directly beneath its body, which suggests it was a fast-moving predator despite its bulky size.

Tr	Middle Triassic
Size:	10 ft/3 m long
Order:	Archosauria
Family:	Rauisuchidae
Range:	Europe: Switzerland
Pronunciation:	ti-SIEN-oh-SOOK-us

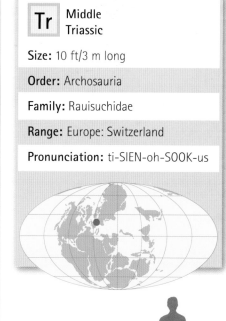

Tr	Early Triassic
Size:	6 ft 6 in/2 m long
Order:	Archosauria
Family:	Erythrosuchidae
Range:	Africa: South Africa
Pronunciation:	er-ITH-ro-SOOK-us

Erythrosuchus

Ticinosuchus

Ticinosuchus' back was protected by two rows of small, bony plates. Its tail was also covered with armor above and below. With its hind legs held almost directly beneath its body, *Ticinosuchus* was well adapted for walking on land. More importantly, part of one of its foot bones had developed into a heel. This meant that its feet were more flexible and it did not need the long toes of earlier reptiles to push its feet off the ground.

Ticinosuchus

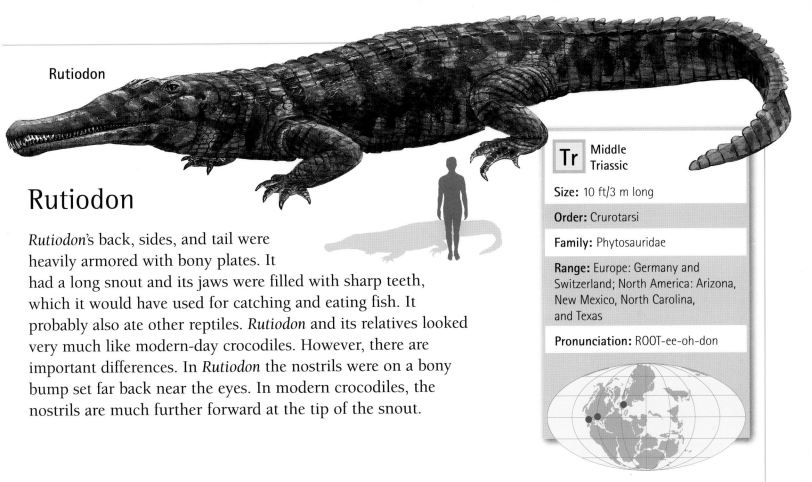

Rutiodon

Rutiodon's back, sides, and tail were
heavily armored with bony plates. It
had a long snout and its jaws were filled with sharp teeth,
which it would have used for catching and eating fish. It
probably also ate other reptiles. *Rutiodon* and its relatives looked
very much like modern-day crocodiles. However, there are
important differences. In *Rutiodon* the nostrils were on a bony
bump set far back near the eyes. In modern crocodiles, the
nostrils are much further forward at the tip of the snout.

Tr	**Middle Triassic**
Size:	10 ft/3 m long
Order:	Crurotarsi
Family:	Phytosauridae
Range:	Europe: Germany and Switzerland; North America: Arizona, New Mexico, North Carolina, and Texas
Pronunciation:	ROOT-ee-oh-don

Stagonolepis

Stagonolepis

Stagonolepis was a slow-moving plant-eater.
It had heavy body armor to protect itself
from attack by its quicker, meat-eating relatives.
Stagonolepis had a small head for its size, only 10 in
(25 cm) long. It had no teeth at the front of its jaws,
but the peglike teeth at the back were good for
eating tough plants such as
horsetails, ferns, and cycads. The
snout was flat and piglike, a good
shape for rooting through small bushes.

Tr	**Late Triassic**
Size:	10 ft/3 m long
Order:	Archosauria
Family:	Stagonolepididae
Range:	Europe: Scotland
Pronunciation:	STAG-oh-no-LEP-is

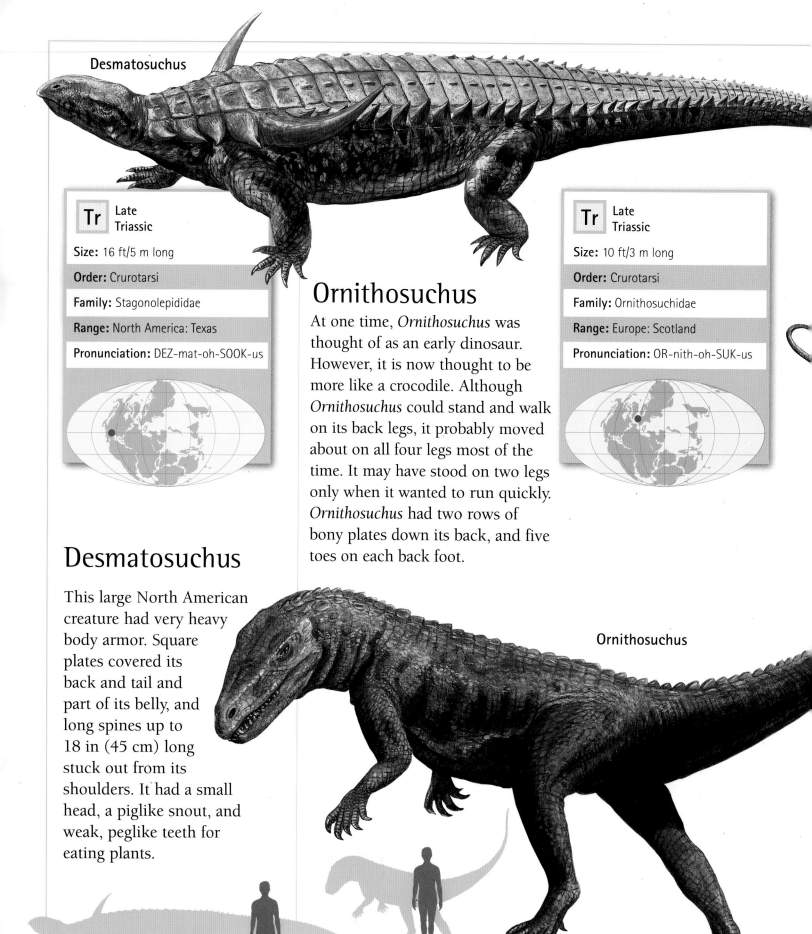

Desmatosuchus

Tr	Late Triassic

Size: 16 ft/5 m long

Order: Crurotarsi

Family: Stagonolepididae

Range: North America: Texas

Pronunciation: DEZ-mat-oh-SOOK-us

Ornithosuchus

At one time, *Ornithosuchus* was thought of as an early dinosaur. However, it is now thought to be more like a crocodile. Although *Ornithosuchus* could stand and walk on its back legs, it probably moved about on all four legs most of the time. It may have stood on two legs only when it wanted to run quickly. *Ornithosuchus* had two rows of bony plates down its back, and five toes on each back foot.

Tr	Late Triassic

Size: 10 ft/3 m long

Order: Crurotarsi

Family: Ornithosuchidae

Range: Europe: Scotland

Pronunciation: OR-nith-oh-SUK-us

Desmatosuchus

This large North American creature had very heavy body armor. Square plates covered its back and tail and part of its belly, and long spines up to 18 in (45 cm) long stuck out from its shoulders. It had a small head, a piglike snout, and weak, peglike teeth for eating plants.

Ornithosuchus

Lagosuchus

Lagosuchus had hind legs very like those of the dinosaurs. Its back legs were long and slim and the shin bones were almost twice the length of the thigh bones. This meant that, when it needed to, *Lagosuchus* could have stood up and run very fast on just on its hind legs.

Tr	Middle Triassic

Size: 1 ft/30 cm long

Order: Dinosauromorpha

Family: Ornithosuchidae

Range: South America: Argentina

Pronunciation: LAG-oh-SOOK-us

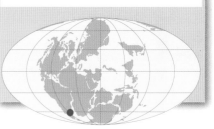

Lagosuchus

Longisquama

Longisquama was a strange lizard-like creature. Paleontologists cannot connect it to any of the known families in this group of early reptiles. Its body was covered in overlapping scales. An amazing row of tall, stiff scales also rose up from its back. What these were for, no one is sure. They could have been for display—used to attract a mate or scare off enemies. They may also have helped to regulate *Longisquama*'s body temperature by attracting heat when the creature was cold, or giving off heat when it was too warm. It has also been suggested that the scales helped the creature to glide through the air. It is not certain whether they could be folded down.

Tr	Early Triassic

Size: 6 in/15 cm long

Order: Uncertain

Family: Uncertain

Range: Europe: Scotland

Pronunciation: LONG-ee-SKWA-ma

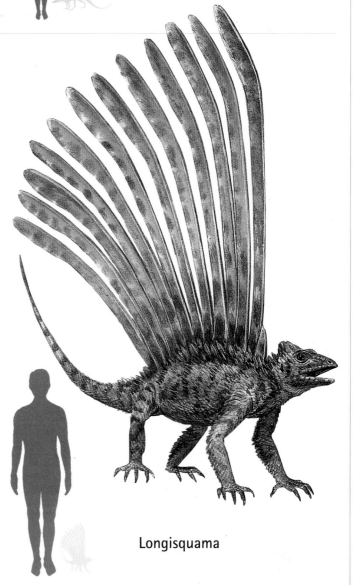

Longisquama

Crocodiles

The crocodiles and their relatives are the only survivors of the archosaurs, or ruling reptiles, alive today. Crocodiles have changed little since they first appeared some 230 million years ago. Although today's crocodiles are more at home in water than on land, they started out as small meat-eaters that could run on their long, slim back legs. Like today's crocodiles, early crocodiles had long, massive skulls and powerful jaws that could snap shut. The jaw muscles attached far back on the skull so that the animal could open its jaws wide.

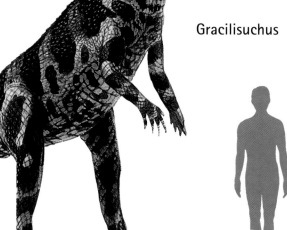

Gracilisuchus

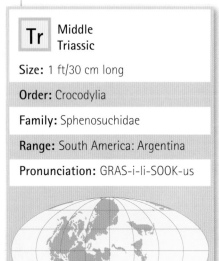

Tr	Middle Triassic

Size: 1 ft/30 cm long

Order: Crocodylia

Family: Sphenosuchidae

Range: South America: Argentina

Pronunciation: GRAS-i-li-SOOK-us

Gracilisuchus

This tiny creature had a light body and a large head. It could run standing up on its slim hind legs. However, it was still a crocodile. *Gracilisuchus* lived on the land, and it was protected by two rows of bony plates that ran down its back to the tip of the tail. It probably chased after small lizards, killing them in its powerful jaws.

Terrestrisuchus

Terrestrisuchus was smaller than *Gracilisuchus* (left). Its body was short, but its tail was almost twice the length of its body and head put together. Like *Gracilisuchus*, *Terrestrisuchus* had long legs and must have sprinted over the dry landscape, snapping up insects and small lizards in its long jaws. It probably ran mostly on four legs, but could have run even faster on just its back legs, using its tail for balance.

Terrestrisuchus

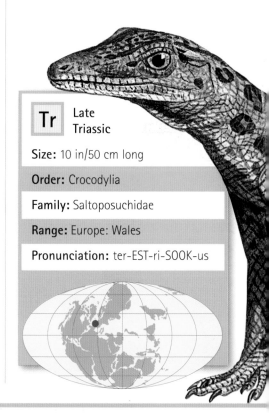

Tr	Late Triassic

Size: 10 in/50 cm long

Order: Crocodylia

Family: Saltoposuchidae

Range: Europe: Wales

Pronunciation: ter-EST-ri-SOOK-us

Protosuchus

Protosuchus

Protosuchus lived on the land, but its skull was similar to modern water-dwelling crocodiles. It had short jaws that became very wide at the back of the skull. This means that the jaw muscles would have been large, so that *Protosuchus* could open its mouth very wide and bite down with a lot of force. A pair of long canine teeth at the front of the lower jaw fitted into notches on either side of the upper jaw when the mouth was closed. Modern crocodiles have similar teeth.

Ju	Early Jurassic
Size: 3 ft 3 in/1 m long	
Order: Crocodylia	
Family: Protosuchidae	
Range: North America: Arizona	
Pronunciation: PROE-toh-SOOK-us	

Pristichampsus

Pristichampsus had long legs that were good for running. Its feet had hooves instead of claws, which also helped it to move more easily on land. *Pristichampsus* had the teeth of a meat-eater and would have fed on the many mammals that appeared on the planet in Eocene times. The teeth were sharp and flattened from side to side with saw-edges, rather like steak knives. Its teeth were almost identical to those of the largest carnivorous dinosaurs, such as *Tyrannosaurus* or *Albertosaurus* (see pp.96–97).

Eo	Eocene

Size: 10 ft/3 m long

Order: Crocodylia

Family: Pristichampsidae

Range: Europe: Germany; North America: Wyoming

Pronunciation: PRIS-ti-CAMP-sus

Deinosuchus

Cr	Late Cretaceous

Size: 49 ft/15 m long

Order: Crocodylia

Family: Alligatoridae

Range: North America: Texas

Pronunciation: DINE-oh-SOOK-us

Deinosuchus

Only the skull of this immense crocodile has been found. On its own the skull measured more than 6 ft 6 in (2 m) in length, which means that if *Deinosuchus* had the same body proportions as other crocodiles, it would have been just under 50 ft (15 m) long! It lived in swamps and probably ambushed passing dinosaurs by lying very still and then grabbing its prey.

Pristichampsus

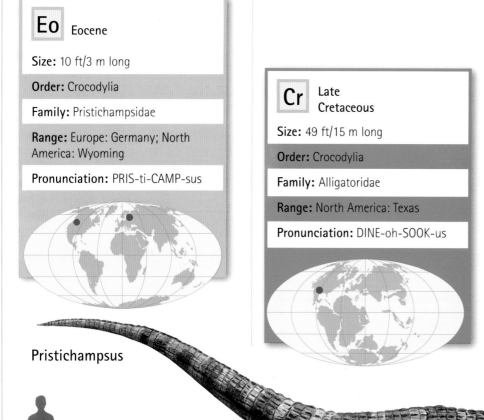

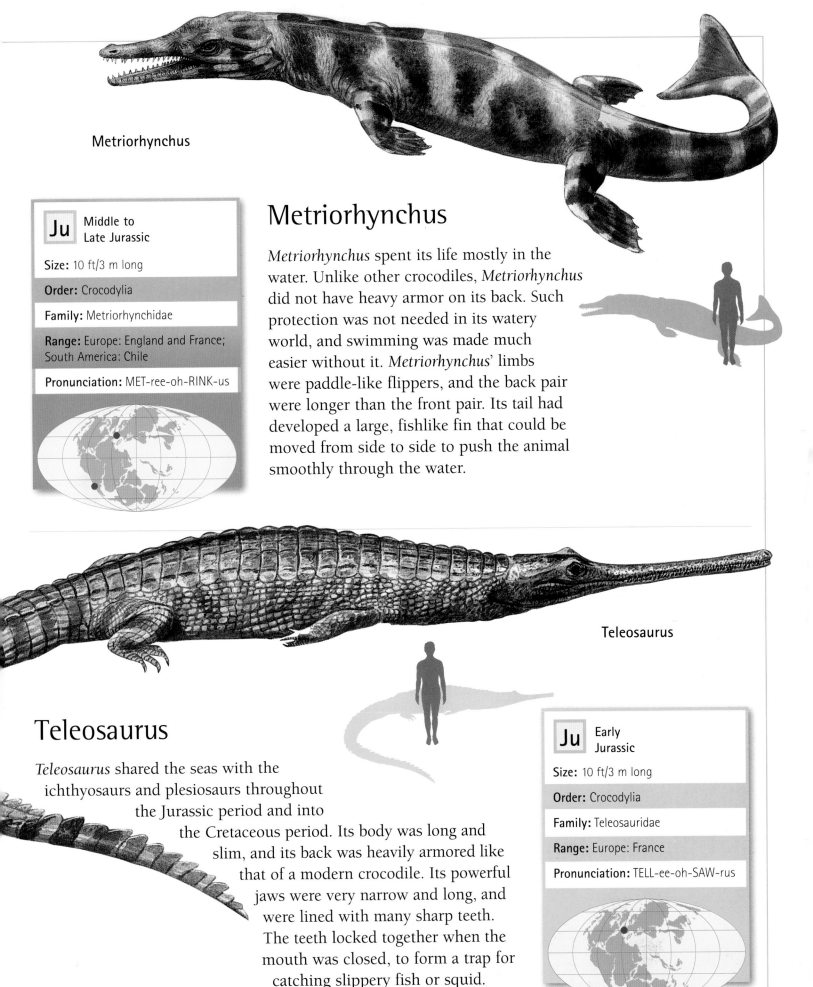

Metriorhynchus

Metriorhynchus

Ju	Middle to Late Jurassic

Size: 10 ft/3 m long

Order: Crocodylia

Family: Metriorhynchidae

Range: Europe: England and France; South America: Chile

Pronunciation: MET-ree-oh-RINK-us

Metriorhynchus spent its life mostly in the water. Unlike other crocodiles, *Metriorhynchus* did not have heavy armor on its back. Such protection was not needed in its watery world, and swimming was made much easier without it. *Metriorhynchus'* limbs were paddle-like flippers, and the back pair were longer than the front pair. Its tail had developed a large, fishlike fin that could be moved from side to side to push the animal smoothly through the water.

Teleosaurus

Teleosaurus

Teleosaurus shared the seas with the ichthyosaurs and plesiosaurs throughout the Jurassic period and into the Cretaceous period. Its body was long and slim, and its back was heavily armored like that of a modern crocodile. Its powerful jaws were very narrow and long, and were lined with many sharp teeth. The teeth locked together when the mouth was closed, to form a trap for catching slippery fish or squid.

Ju	Early Jurassic

Size: 10 ft/3 m long

Order: Crocodylia

Family: Teleosauridae

Range: Europe: France

Pronunciation: TELL-ee-oh-SAW-rus

Life in Jurassic Skies

By 200 million years ago, reptiles had taken to the skies. The early flying reptiles—called pterosaurs—flew on leathery wings and had powerful jaws and sharp claws. They dominated life in the air and thrived throughout the Jurassic period. In the Late Jurassic period, the first bird appeared.

Birdlike Dinosaur: Compsognathus

This tiny, chicken-sized creature only weighed about 8 lb (3.6 kg). *Compsognathus* must have been a fast hunter. Its bones were hollow, which meant it was lightweight; it had a long neck and a long tail for balance; and it could run quickly on its two long-shinned hind legs. *Compsognathus* had short arms with two pincer-like fingers. It also had birdlike feet with three clawed toes and a fourth toe that pointed backward.

Right: The waters of a shallow lagoon 250 million years ago in southern Germany were good hunting grounds for small reptiles such as *Compsognathus*. Many flying pterosaurs also hunted there. These included the long-toothed, fish-eating *Rhamphorhynchus* and the smaller *Pterodactylus*, which may have caught insects as it was flying. Most famous of all is the early bird called *Archaeopteryx*. It had a long tail and probably could not fly very well.

Pterodactylus

Dragonfly

Rhamphorhychus

Compsagnathus

In Late Jurassic times there was a large lagoon in a part of what is now southern Germany. The bodies of land animals and plants were washed into the water and settled on the lagoon bed. There they were covered with chalky mud and over time turned into fossils. The remains of dragonflies, flying pterosaurs, small dinosaurs, and, most famous of all, *Archaeopteryx* have been found.

Archaeopteryx flew through the air alongside the flying reptiles. The earliest pterosaurs appeared during the Late Triassic period. Their hollow, light skeletons were ideal for flight. The smaller species of pterosaurs had wingspans of up to 16 in (40 cm) and probably fed on insects. The larger species were fish-eaters, diving to scoop their prey out of the sea. Their wingspan grew as large as 40 ft (12 m).

Early Bird: Archaeopteryx

Archaeopteryx was classified as the first bird. It was about the size of a modern pigeon. It had a small head and large eyes, pointed teeth, and a long bony tail. Its limbs were long and slender, with three claws on each hand. Like a modern bird, it had feathers on its arms and tail. Most paleontologists believe that *Archaeopteryx* ate insects, and could fly or glide from tree to tree. From time to time it would have landed on the ground and used its sharp claws to climb back into the trees.

Archaeopteryx

Compsagnathus

75

Flying Reptiles

The first group of vertebrates to take to the air were the pterosaurs. These flying reptiles flew on "wings" made of skin. They evolved in Late Triassic times, some 70 million years before the first known bird, *Archaeopteryx*, appeared. The earliest known pterosaurs were already good flyers by around 190 million years ago and were the largest flying creatures of all time. By 65 million years ago, however, they had all died out. Pterosaur remains have been found all over the world, except in Antarctica. The most famous of these flying reptiles were the pterodactyls.

Ju	Early Jurassic
Size: 4 ft/1.2 m wingspan	
Order: Pterosauria	
Family: Dimorphodontidae	
Range: Europe: England	
Pronunciation: die-MORF-oh-don	

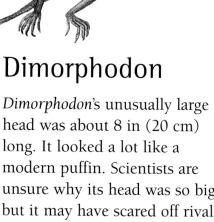

Dimorphodon

Eudimorphodon

Eudimorphodon had a short neck and a bony tail that was about half its length. The head was large, but light. The flaps of skin that made up its wings stretched from the enormously long fourth finger of each hand to the side of the body at the thighs.

Tr	Late Triassic
Size: 2 ft 5 in/75 cm wingspan	
Order: Pterosauria	
Family: Eudimorphodontidae	
Range: Europe: Italy	
Pronunciation: yoo-DIE-morf-oh-don	

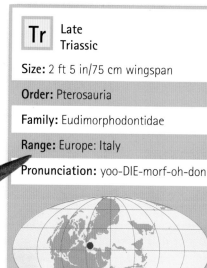

Dimorphodon

Dimorphodon's unusually large head was about 8 in (20 cm) long. It looked a lot like a modern puffin. Scientists are unsure why its head was so big, but it may have scared off rivals or attracted mates. *Dimorphodon* may have used its clawed fingers and toes to hang from cliffs or branches like a bat before launching into the air.

Eudimorphodon

Rhamphorhynchus

Rhamphorhynchus' wings were made of very thin skin. Similar to the wings of a modern bat, its wings were strengthened by thin fibers running from the front to the back. *Rhamphorhynchus* had long, narrow jaws filled with sharp teeth that pointed outward. These teeth were used to snatch fish from out of the water. When hunting, *Rhamphorhynchus* probably flew only a few inches above the surface of the water. It would hold its long tail out to keep its balance. As soon as it saw a fish, it would snap the prey up in its jaws.

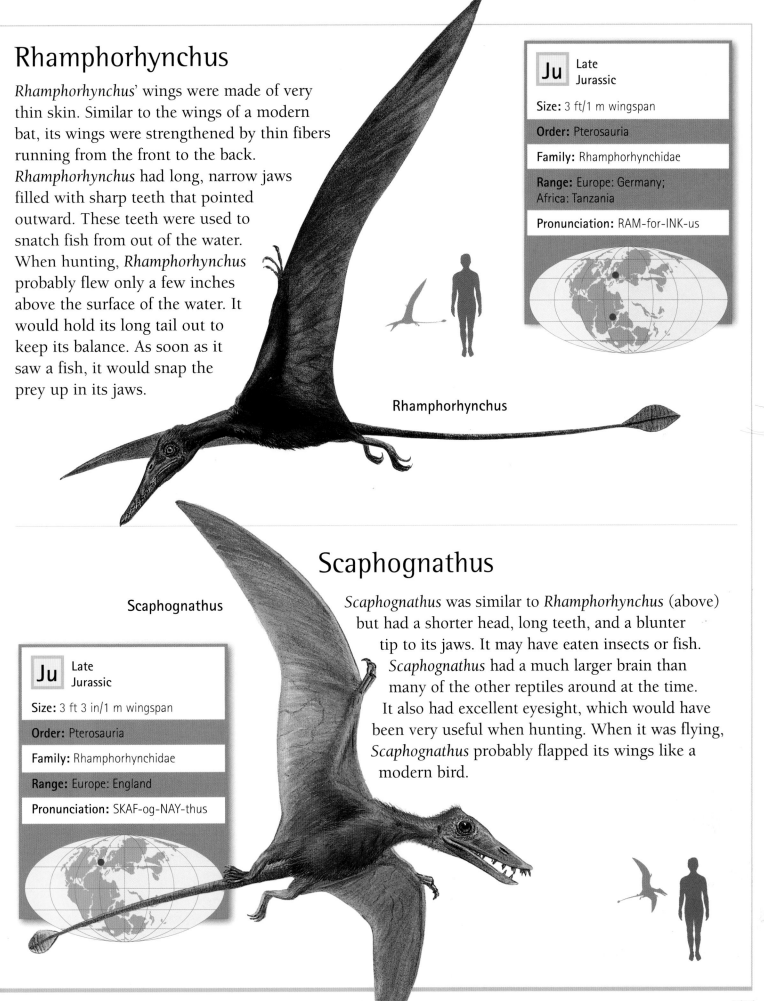

Ju	Late Jurassic
Size: 3 ft/1 m wingspan	
Order: Pterosauria	
Family: Rhamphorhynchidae	
Range: Europe: Germany; Africa: Tanzania	
Pronunciation: RAM-for-INK-us	

Rhamphorhynchus

Scaphognathus

Scaphognathus

Scaphognathus was similar to *Rhamphorhynchus* (above) but had a shorter head, long teeth, and a blunter tip to its jaws. It may have eaten insects or fish. *Scaphognathus* had a much larger brain than many of the other reptiles around at the time. It also had excellent eyesight, which would have been very useful when hunting. When it was flying, *Scaphognathus* probably flapped its wings like a modern bird.

Ju	Late Jurassic
Size: 3 ft 3 in/1 m wingspan	
Order: Pterosauria	
Family: Rhamphorhynchidae	
Range: Europe: England	
Pronunciation: SKAF-og-NAY-thus	

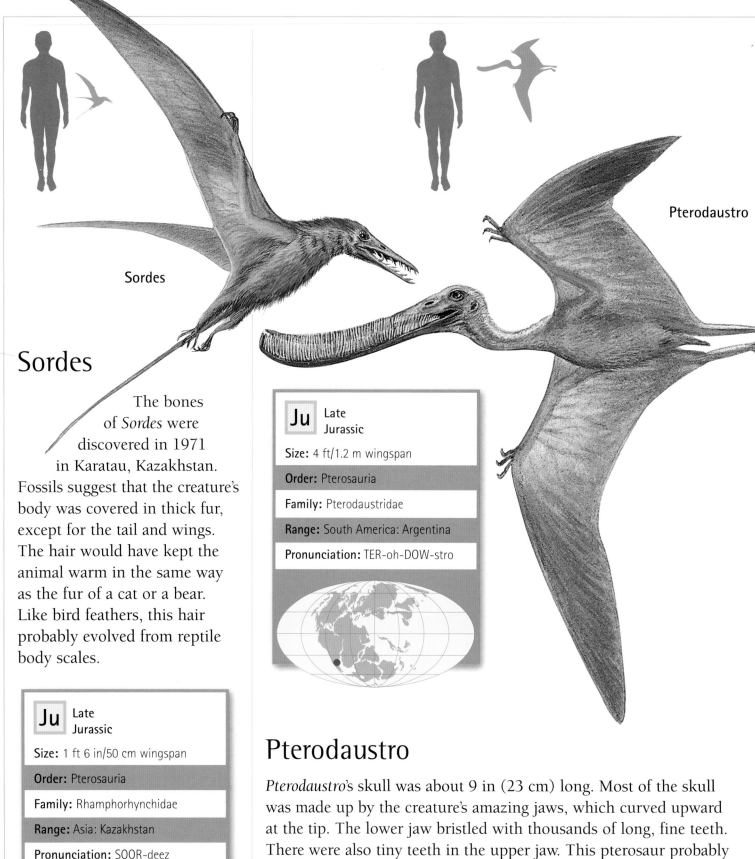

Sordes

Pterodaustro

Sordes

The bones of *Sordes* were discovered in 1971 in Karatau, Kazakhstan. Fossils suggest that the creature's body was covered in thick fur, except for the tail and wings. The hair would have kept the animal warm in the same way as the fur of a cat or a bear. Like bird feathers, this hair probably evolved from reptile body scales.

Ju	Late Jurassic
Size: 1 ft 6 in/50 cm wingspan	
Order: Pterosauria	
Family: Rhamphorhynchidae	
Range: Asia: Kazakhstan	
Pronunciation: SOOR-deez	

Ju	Late Jurassic
Size: 4 ft/1.2 m wingspan	
Order: Pterosauria	
Family: Pterodaustridae	
Range: South America: Argentina	
Pronunciation: TER-oh-DOW-stro	

Pterodaustro

Pterodaustro's skull was about 9 in (23 cm) long. Most of the skull was made up by the creature's amazing jaws, which curved upward at the tip. The lower jaw bristled with thousands of long, fine teeth. There were also tiny teeth in the upper jaw. This pterosaur probably fed by skimming along the surface of the sea with its mouth open. As the water flowed through its jaws, tiny water animals, called plankton, would become trapped by the sievelike teeth. Today, some whales have a similar way of feeding.

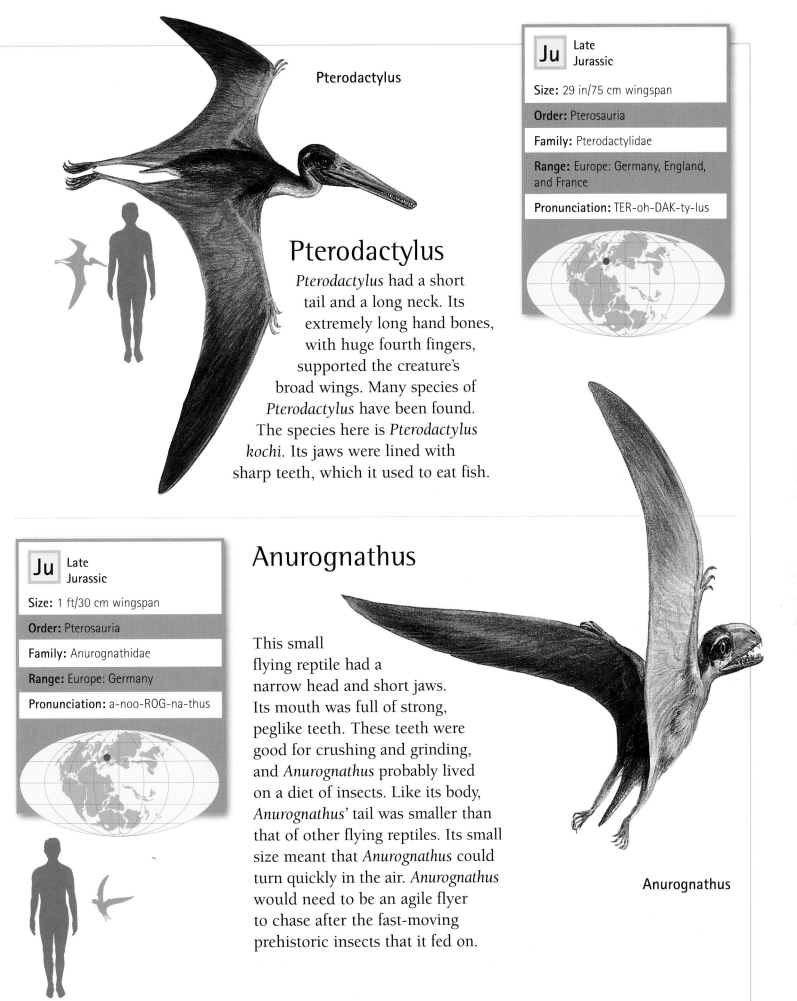

Pterodactylus

Pterodactylus

Pterodactylus had a short tail and a long neck. Its extremely long hand bones, with huge fourth fingers, supported the creature's broad wings. Many species of *Pterodactylus* have been found. The species here is *Pterodactylus kochi*. Its jaws were lined with sharp teeth, which it used to eat fish.

Anurognathus

This small flying reptile had a narrow head and short jaws. Its mouth was full of strong, peglike teeth. These teeth were good for crushing and grinding, and *Anurognathus* probably lived on a diet of insects. Like its body, *Anurognathus'* tail was smaller than that of other flying reptiles. Its small size meant that *Anurognathus* could turn quickly in the air. *Anurognathus* would need to be an agile flyer to chase after the fast-moving prehistoric insects that it fed on.

Anurognathus

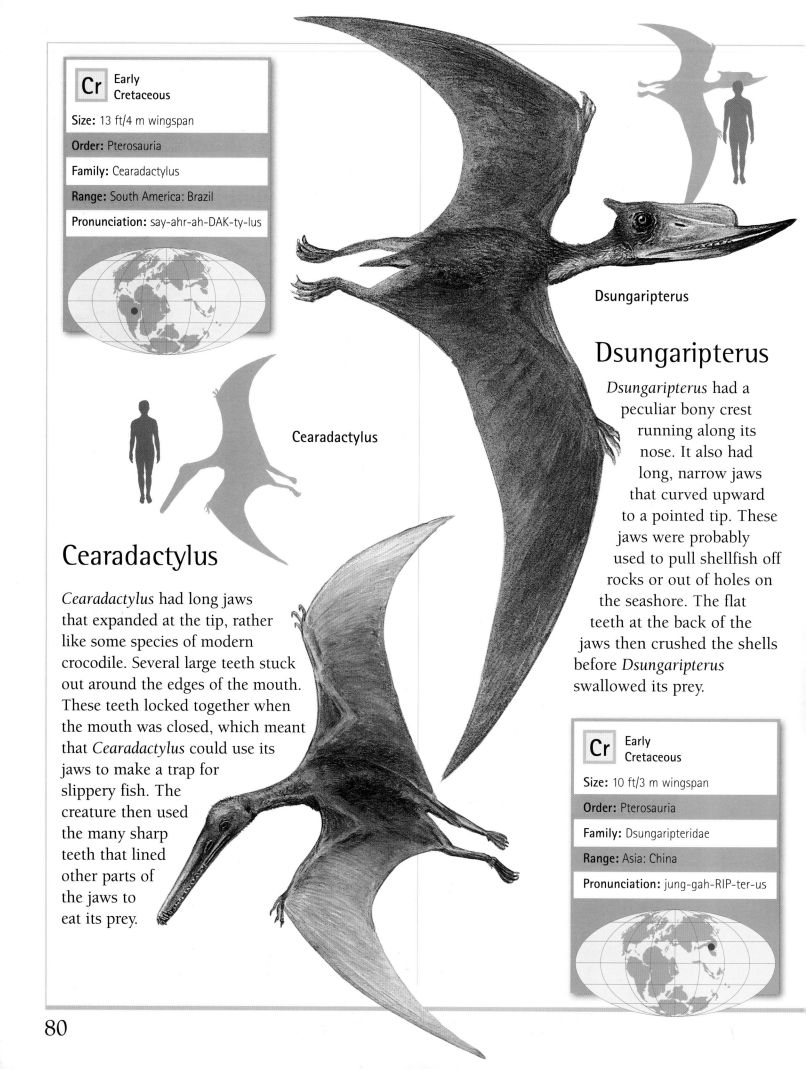

Cr Early Cretaceous

Size: 13 ft/4 m wingspan

Order: Pterosauria

Family: Cearadactylus

Range: South America: Brazil

Pronunciation: say-ahr-ah-DAK-ty-lus

Dsungaripterus

Dsungaripterus

Dsungaripterus had a peculiar bony crest running along its nose. It also had long, narrow jaws that curved upward to a pointed tip. These jaws were probably used to pull shellfish off rocks or out of holes on the seashore. The flat teeth at the back of the jaws then crushed the shells before *Dsungaripterus* swallowed its prey.

Cearadactylus

Cearadactylus

Cearadactylus had long jaws that expanded at the tip, rather like some species of modern crocodile. Several large teeth stuck out around the edges of the mouth. These teeth locked together when the mouth was closed, which meant that *Cearadactylus* could use its jaws to make a trap for slippery fish. The creature then used the many sharp teeth that lined other parts of the jaws to eat its prey.

Cr Early Cretaceous

Size: 10 ft/3 m wingspan

Order: Pterosauria

Family: Dsungaripteridae

Range: Asia: China

Pronunciation: jung-gah-RIP-ter-us

Pteranodon

Pteranodon had a huge wing span and would have been a skillful flyer, gliding through the air like a fighter jet. It had a giant crest on the back of its head. This may have balanced or steered its short, heavy body in the air. Its jaws were not like those of most pterosaurs—they had no teeth. *Pteranodon* probably fed like a modern pelican, scooping up fish in its jaws and swallowing them whole.

Cr Late Cretaceous

Size: 23 ft/7 m wingspan

Order: Pterosauria

Family: Pteranodontidae

Range: Europe: England; North America: Kansas

Pronunciation: te-RAN-oh-don

Pteranodon

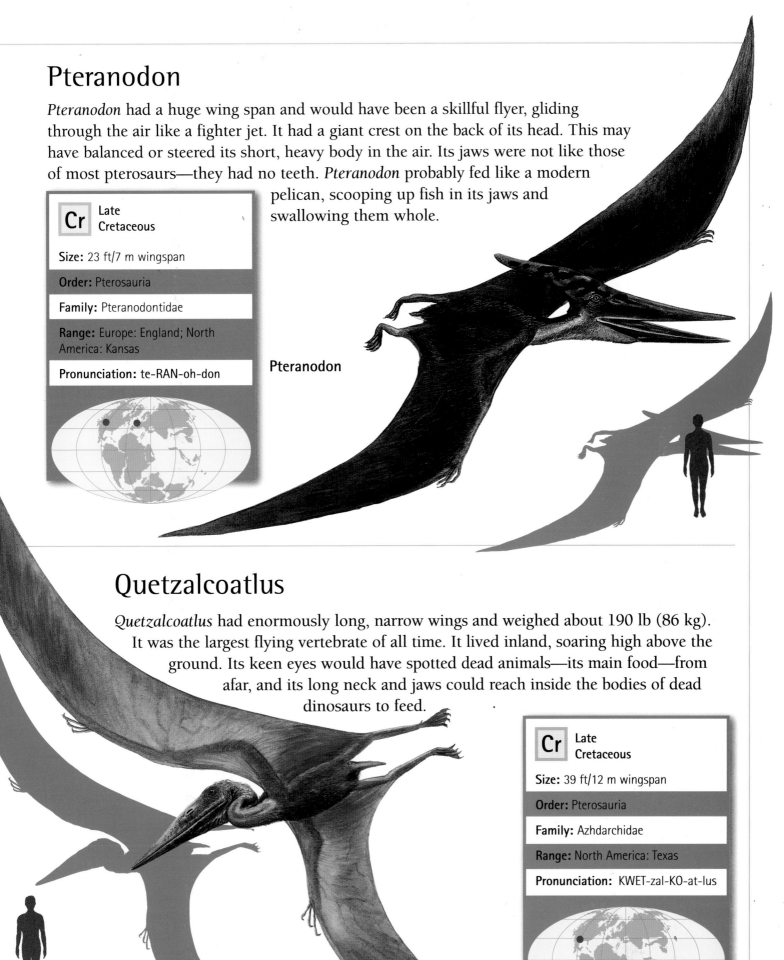

Quetzalcoatlus

Quetzalcoatlus had enormously long, narrow wings and weighed about 190 lb (86 kg). It was the largest flying vertebrate of all time. It lived inland, soaring high above the ground. Its keen eyes would have spotted dead animals—its main food—from afar, and its long neck and jaws could reach inside the bodies of dead dinosaurs to feed.

Cr Late Cretaceous

Size: 39 ft/12 m wingspan

Order: Pterosauria

Family: Azhdarchidae

Range: North America: Texas

Pronunciation: KWET-zal-KO-at-lus

Dinosaur Discovery

Dinosaur fossils are sometimes found by accident. More often, they are discovered by members of scientific expeditions. Paleontologists know in which types and ages of rock to look for fossils. When a fossil is found, each bone must be cleaned and preserved before a skeleton can be rebuilt. This reconstruction can sometimes take years.

Digging for Dinosaurs

Hunting for fossils takes time and money. Some trips take years to plan. Today's paleontologists usually head for places in the world where they know that fossils are common. Once a skeleton has been found, the first job is to get it under cover. After lying in the ground for millions of years, the bones are usually cracked and delicate. First, the rock lying above the bones is carefully removed. Then pieces of rock surrounding the bones are cut out of the ground. Each fossil is wrapped in strips of cloth soaked in plaster of Paris to protect it. Before they are removed from the rock, the bones are measured and photographed. This information helps scientists work out how the bones may have fitted together in a complete skeleton and even how the animal died.

Loose fragments of rock or soft clay are removed by hand or with soft brushes.

The scientists make plans of the site, showing the position of each bone.

Freeing a skeleton from rock takes a team of people, working with such tools as pneumatic drills, pickaxes, and soft brushes.

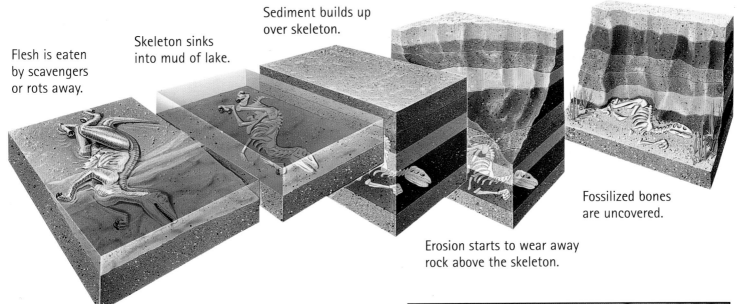

Flesh is eaten by scavengers or rots away.

Skeleton sinks into mud of lake.

Sediment builds up over skeleton.

Erosion starts to wear away rock above the skeleton.

Fossilized bones are uncovered.

How a Fossil Forms

Imagine a dinosaur dies by the bank of a muddy lake. Its flesh is eaten or rots away. As the years pass, the skeleton sinks into the earth. Minerals slowly turn the soft surrounding mud into hard rock. They also replace the minerals in the bones of the skeleton, turning them into stone. These stone remains are fossils. Skin was usually eaten, or rotted away with a dinosaur's other soft body parts, but sometimes scientists find rocks with prints of dinosaur skin in them. Teeth are covered with hard enamel and survive well as fossils. Scientists have also found many fossilized dinosaur eggs. Some even contain small skeletons.

Paleontologist Dr. Barnum Brown examines dinosaur bones found in a dry lake in Wyoming, August 9, 1934.

Building a Skeleton

Putting a dinosaur skeleton together is called reconstruction. Paleontologists study each bone of a dinosaur very carefully to work out how its skeleton fits together. They then make drawings to show how muscles probably moved the bones, by using evidence from the surface of each bone, and by comparing them to present-day animals. Once they have a good idea of the shape and size of a dinosaur, they can imagine what it looked like when the muscle was covered with skin. They must also decide whether the animal had horny claws, feathers, or lips. This is very difficult, as all these body parts do not fossilize easily. They must also decide what color the dinosaur may have been.

Only about 60 percent of the bones of Baryonyx, a dinosaur discovered in Britain in 1983, were ever found.

■ Fossil bones
□ Reconstructed bones

Birdlike Dinosaurs

Paleontologists believe that birds evolved from small dinosaurs that could run upright on their long, slim back legs. Ornithomimids, or birdlike dinosaurs, were similar in size and shape to the modern ostrich, except they had long arms that each had three powerful fingers. Ornithomimids could run at speeds of 22–37 mph (35–60 km/h). They probably traveled the plains in groups, looking after their young while on the move. They had horny, birdlike beaks instead of teeth, which they used to snap up small animals and insects.

Coelurus

Ornithomimus

This ostrich dinosaur had a small head with a large brain, no teeth, and beaklike jaws. *Ornithomimus* would have sprinted along with its body parallel to the ground, balanced by its extra-long tail. It probably ate leaves, fruit, insects, and small animals, such as lizards.

Cr	Late Cretaceous
Size: 11 ft 6 in/3.5 m long	
Order: Saurischia	
Family: Ornithomimidae	
Range: North America: Colorado and Montana; Asia: Tibet	
Pronunciation: or-NITH-oh-MEEM-us	

Coelurus

Coelurus had a small, low head that was only about 8 in (20 cm) long. Its birdlike bones were hollow, like those of many of the early dinosaurs. *Coelurus* lived in the forests and swamps of North America, where it was an active predator. It ran about on its long legs to hunt down small animals, and used its strong hands, each of which had three long, clawed fingers to grab its prey.

Ju	Late Jurassic
Size: 6 ft 6 in/2 m long	
Order: Saurischia	
Family: Coeluridae	
Range: North America: Wyoming	
Pronunciation: see-LOO-rus	

Ornithomimus

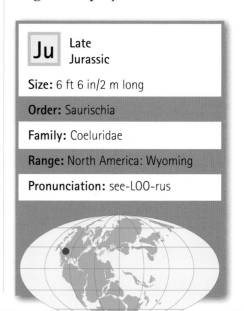

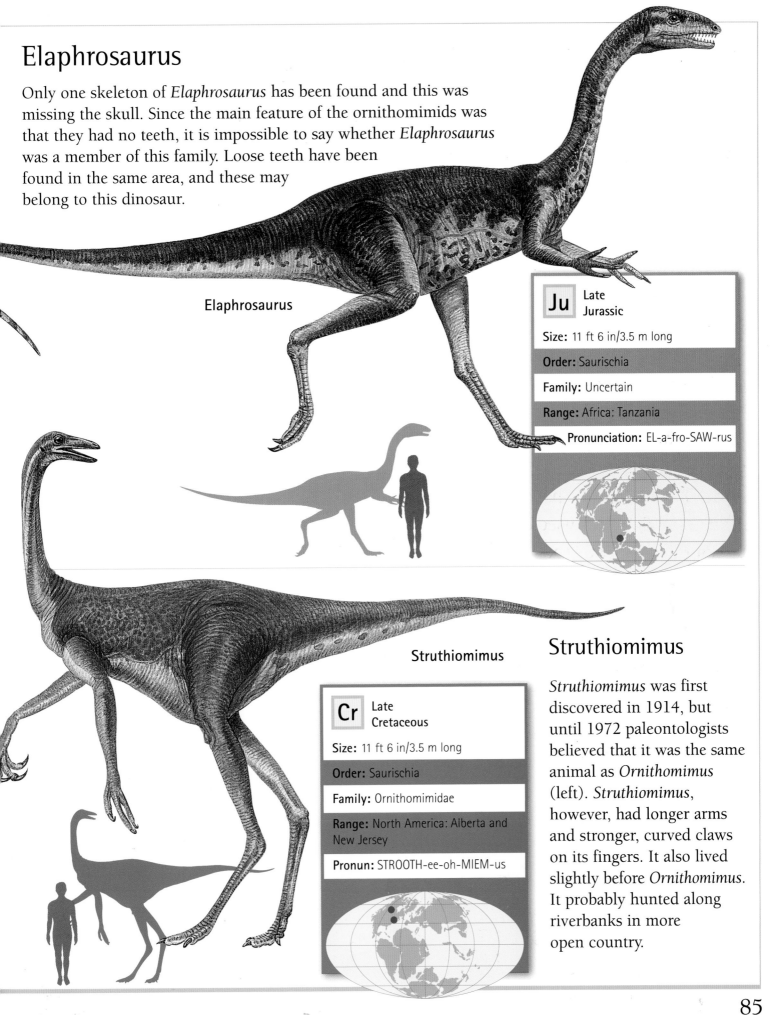

Elaphrosaurus

Only one skeleton of *Elaphrosaurus* has been found and this was missing the skull. Since the main feature of the ornithomimids was that they had no teeth, it is impossible to say whether *Elaphrosaurus* was a member of this family. Loose teeth have been found in the same area, and these may belong to this dinosaur.

Elaphrosaurus

Ju	Late Jurassic
Size: 11 ft 6 in/3.5 m long	
Order: Saurischia	
Family: Uncertain	
Range: Africa: Tanzania	
Pronunciation: EL-a-fro-SAW-rus	

Struthiomimus

Struthiomimus

Cr	Late Cretaceous
Size: 11 ft 6 in/3.5 m long	
Order: Saurischia	
Family: Ornithomimidae	
Range: North America: Alberta and New Jersey	
Pronun: STROOTH-ee-oh-MIEM-us	

Struthiomimus was first discovered in 1914, but until 1972 paleontologists believed that it was the same animal as *Ornithomimus* (left). *Struthiomimus*, however, had longer arms and stronger, curved claws on its fingers. It also lived slightly before *Ornithomimus*. It probably hunted along riverbanks in more open country.

Oviraptor

This animal had a skull that was different from that of any other dinosaur. The head was almost parrot-like—short and deep, with a stumpy beak and no teeth. Powerful jaw muscles, however, gave the beak enough power to crush objects as hard as bones. *Oviraptor*'s body was like many small, flesh-eating dinosaurs. It had three grasping fingers on each hand, and each nail was about 3 in (8 cm) long. The animal walked on its two long, slender legs. The body was balanced by the long tail. The first *Oviraptor* specimen was found in 1924. In the 1990s, specimens of *Oviraptor* mothers were discovered that had been buried in a sandstorm while sitting on their nests and unhatched eggs.

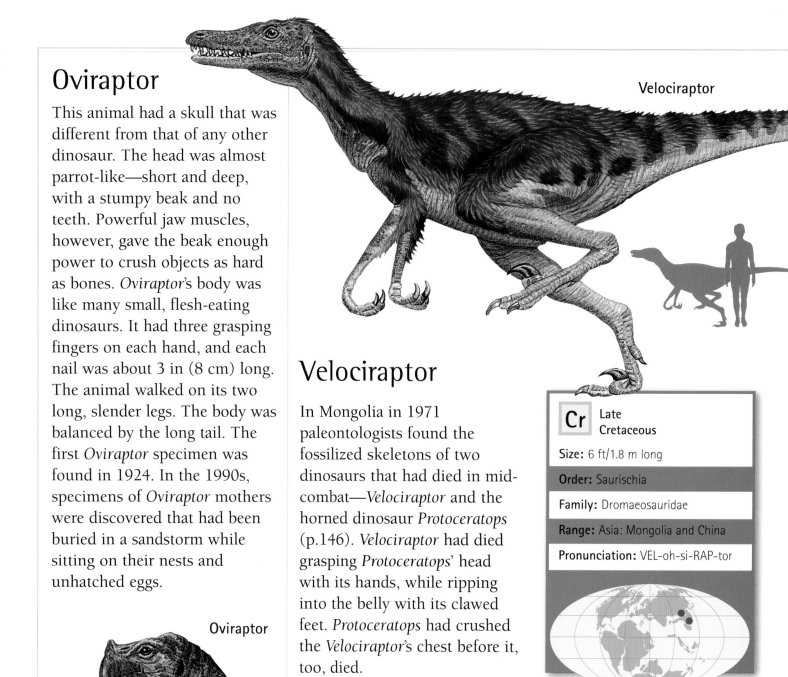

Velociraptor

Velociraptor

In Mongolia in 1971 paleontologists found the fossilized skeletons of two dinosaurs that had died in mid-combat—*Velociraptor* and the horned dinosaur *Protoceratops* (p.146). *Velociraptor* had died grasping *Protoceratops*' head with its hands, while ripping into the belly with its clawed feet. *Protoceratops* had crushed the *Velociraptor*'s chest before it, too, died.

Cr	Late Cretaceous
Size: 6 ft/1.8 m long	
Order: Saurischia	
Family: Dromaeosauridae	
Range: Asia: Mongolia and China	
Pronunciation: VEL-oh-si-RAP-tor	

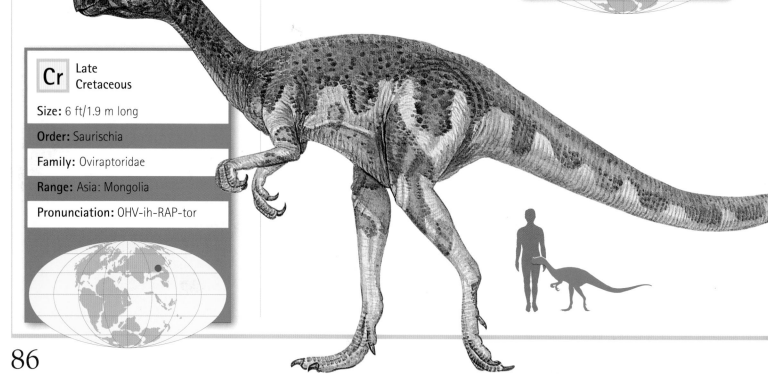

Oviraptor

Cr	Late Cretaceous
Size: 6 ft/1.9 m long	
Order: Saurischia	
Family: Oviraptoridae	
Range: Asia: Mongolia	
Pronunciation: OHV-ih-RAP-tor	

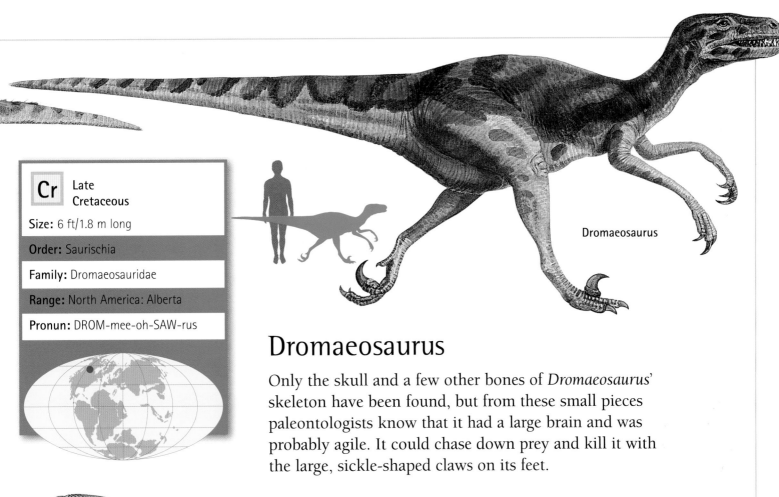

Cr	Late Cretaceous
Size: 6 ft/1.8 m long	
Order: Saurischia	
Family: Dromaeosauridae	
Range: North America: Alberta	
Pronun: DROM-mee-oh-SAW-rus	

Dromaeosaurus

Dromaeosaurus

Only the skull and a few other bones of *Dromaeosaurus'* skeleton have been found, but from these small pieces paleontologists know that it had a large brain and was probably agile. It could chase down prey and kill it with the large, sickle-shaped claws on its feet.

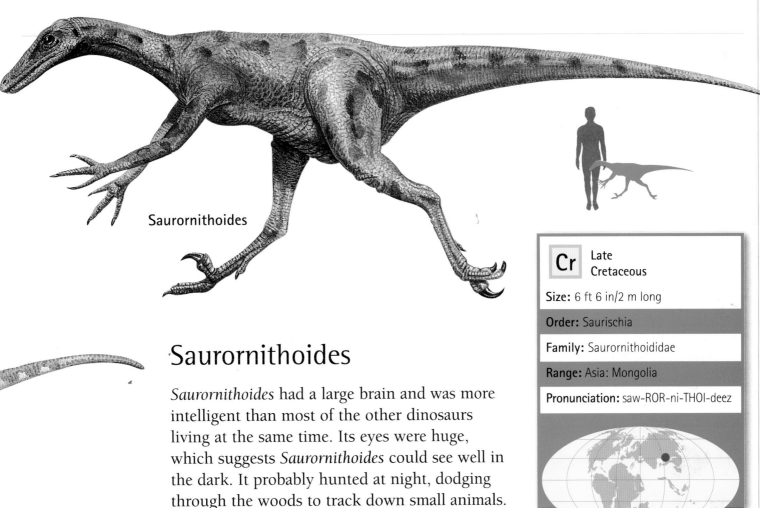

Saurornithoides

Saurornithoides

Saurornithoides had a large brain and was more intelligent than most of the other dinosaurs living at the same time. Its eyes were huge, which suggests *Saurornithoides* could see well in the dark. It probably hunted at night, dodging through the woods to track down small animals.

Cr	Late Cretaceous
Size: 6 ft 6 in/2 m long	
Order: Saurischia	
Family: Saurornithoididae	
Range: Asia: Mongolia	
Pronunciation: saw-ROR-ni-THOI-deez	

Therizinosaurus

Only a few fossils of *Therizinosaurus* have been found so far. They show a creature with arms that had huge sickle-shaped claws that were more than 27 in (70 cm) long. The dinosaur may have used these claws to gather leaves and pass them to its toothless beak.

Therizinosaurus

Cr Early Cretaceous

Size: 6 ft/2 m long

Order: Saurischia

Family: Ornithomimidae

Range: Europe: Spain

Pronunciation: pel-e-KAN-I-MEEM-us

Pelicanimimus

This was the first ostrich-like dinosaur to be found in Europe. It had a long, narrow skull and it may have had a throat pouch, like a pelican. Unlike other ostrich dinosaurs, *Pelecanimimus* had a large number of teeth in its long jaws—as many as 220.

Pelicanimimus

Cr Late Cretaceous

Size: 13-16 ft/4-5 m long

Order: Saurischia

Family: Therizinosauridae

Range: Asia: Mongolia and China

Pronun: thair-uh-ZEEN-uh-SAW-rus

Alxasaurus

Cr Early
Cretaceous

Size: 13 ft/4 m long

Order: Saurischia

Family: Theirzinosauridae

Range: Asia: Mongolia and China

Pronunciation: AHL-shah-SAW-rus

Alxasaurus had long, slender arms and hands with huge claws. Its body was bulky with large hips and a short tail. It may have used its tail to help prop itself up as it fed. The small head ended in a toothless beak, but there were some small teeth further back in the jaws.

Alxasaurus

Dromiceiomimus

Dromiceiomimus had long, slender legs. Its shin bones were much longer than its thigh bones, which suggests that it was a very fast runner. It also had a large brain, and huge eyes that were good for seeing in the dark. Like *Saurornithoides* (see p.87), *Dromiceiomimus* probably hunted at night, chasing small mammals and lizards through the woods in which it lived.

Dromiceiomimus

Cr Late
Cretaceous

Size: 11.5 ft/3.5 m long

Order: Saurischia

Family: Ornithomimidae

Range: North America: Alberta

Pronun: droh-MEE-see-oh-MEEM-us

Attacking Dinosaurs

The prehistoric world was full of terrifying meat-eating dinosaurs. Some of them, such as the mighty *Tyrannosaurus rex*, were huge. Other killers were much smaller, but the weapons they had on their hands and feet meant they could be just as dangerous.

Just like animals today, meat-eating dinosaurs fought in life and death struggles with their prey. Special weapons, such as powerful claws, sharp teeth, and strong jaws, helped them win their battles. Speed was also important to an attacking dinosaur. Smaller hunters in particular would get close to their victims in high-speed chases before making the final pounce. Larger predators, such as tyrannosaurs, relied on their size and strength to kill their prey.

Hunting in Packs

Smaller hunting dinosaurs such as *Deinonychus* and *Dromaeosaurus* may have hunted in packs. By working together they could bring down huge plant-eaters much larger than themselves. Like hunting dogs today, a group of predators could have surrounded a large dinosaur, some leaping on its back while others slashed at its skin with their sharp claws.

Speedy Hunter: Dromaeosaurus

Dromaeosaurus lived in North America during the Late Cretaceous period. It was a slender-bodied dinosaur that ran fast on two legs—it may have reached speeds of 37 mph (60 km/h) or more. When it caught up with its prey, it leaped off the ground to tear at the victim's flesh using the powerful claws on its back feet. The long tail helped *Dromaeosaurus* balance as it ran and pounced on its prey.

Dromaeosaurus chases prey

Springs toward its victim

Leaps off ground to tear at its prey's flesh

Special Weapons

Dromaeosaurus had a lethal weapon—an extra-large claw on the second toe of each foot. This sharp, sickle-shaped claw was up to 5 in (13 cm) long. When running, *Dromaeosaurus* held these special weapons off the ground so that they did not become damaged or blunt. When *Dromaeosaurus* attacked, it used its powerful claws to slash at its victim.

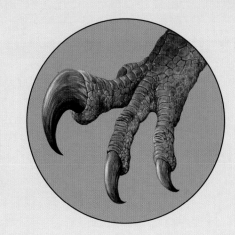

Dromaeosaurus' hands each had three sharp-clawed fingers that it used to seize hold of its prey.

Dinosaur Diets

In the time of the dinosaurs, just like today, there were far more plant-eating animals than meat-eaters. Only the largest hunters, such as tyrannosaurs, would have dared attack the biggest plant-eaters. Even then they would probably have chosen a young or injured animal to attack. The smaller meat-eaters probably caught lizards and insects for most of their food, while dromaeosaurs and their relatives may have hunted in packs to bring down creatures much larger than themselves. At least one dinosaur, the long-jawed *Baryonyx*, may have preyed mostly on fish.

A fast-moving hunter, *Ornitholestes* (left) lived in North America. It probably ate lizards and frogs as well as insects and the earliest birds.

Powerful Jaws

Deinonychus (right) had a large head and extremely powerful jaws. The jaws were lined with backward-curving teeth. Each tooth had a jagged edge like a bread knife for slicing into the flesh of its prey. At 10–13 ft (3–4 m) long, *Deinonychus* was twice as big as its relative *Dromaeosaurus*. It too had a lethal claw on the second toe of each foot.

Theropods

The order of dinosaurs known as the Saurischia can be divided into two groups depending on what they ate. The sauropods were plant-eating dinosaurs with small heads, long necks and tails, massive bodies, and four trunklike legs. The second group were the predatory theropods. These flesh-eating dinosaurs thrived from the Late Triassic to the Late Cretaceous periods. Like sauropods, they were large creatures, but walked on their back legs. The theropods were widespread and make up 40 percent of all known dinosaurs.

Ju	Early Jurassic
Size: 20 ft/6 m long	
Order: Saurischia	
Family: Ceratosauridae	
Range: North America: Arizona	
Pronunciation: die-LOAF-oh-SAW-rus	

Dilophosaurus

Ceratosaurus

Ceratosaurus

Ceratosaurus had powerful jaws armed with sharp, curved teeth. It would have been a fierce hunter. Its arms were short and its hands each had four strong, clawed fingers. Its long legs had three clawed toes on each foot. A row of bony plates ran down the center of *Ceratosaurus'* back and tail, and it had a small horn on its snout.

Ju	Late Jurassic
Size: 20 ft/6 m long	
Order: Saurischia	
Family: Ceratosauridae	
Range: North America: Colorado, and Wyoming	
Pronunciation: SER-a-toe-SAW-rus	

Dilophosaurus

Dilophosaurus was very large, but its bones were long, slender, and light. Its skull had a large bony crest on either side, which narrowed into spikes at the back of the head. Although *Dilophosaurus* had long, sharp teeth, they were probably too thin to bite and kill prey. Instead, *Dilophosaurus* ripped its prey apart with its clawed feet and hands.

Size: 11 ft 6 in/3.5 m long

Order: Saurischia

Family: Megalosauridae

Range: Europe: England

Pronun: yoo-STREP-to-SPON-di-lus

Eustreptospondylus

When the remains of *Eustreptospondylus* were first discovered, many scientists thought that they belonged to another dinosaur called *Megalosaurus* (see p.98). However, a nearly complete skeleton found in 1964 in England showed that *Eustreptospondylus* was in fact a separate animal. The skeleton is now in the University Museum of Oxford. Although parts of its skull are missing, it is the best-preserved specimen of any European carnosaur.

Eustreptospondylus

Proceratosaurus

| Ju | Middle Jurassic |

Size: 16 ft/5 m long

Order: Saurischia

Family: Unknown

Range: Europe: England

Pronunciation: pro-se-RAT-oh-SAW-rus

Proceratosaurus

Only one skull of this fierce carnosaur, or "flesh lizard," has been found. It is similar to the skulls of other carnosaurs, but longer and with a small horn above the snout. *Proceratosaurus* was probably built like other carnosaurs that lived at the time. It had a large head on a short neck and a heavy body. Its long tail was used to keep balance. *Proceratosaurus* had short arms with clawed fingers and long legs for running. Each foot had three toes.

93

Allosaurs and Spinosaurs

Ju–Cr Late Jurassic to Early Cretaceous

Size: 39 ft/12 m long

Order: Saurischia

Family: Allosauridae

Range: North America: Colorado, Utah, and Wyoming; Africa: Tanzania; Australia

Pronunciation: AL-oh-SAW-rus

Allosaurs were the largest meat-eaters on Earth during Late Jurassic times. They lumbered through every continent in the world. Spinosaurs were also huge meat-eating dinosaurs, but they had a more unusual appearance. Some of them had backbones that grew outward to form a crest or "sail" down their backs. Both allosaurs and spinosaurs were soon to be rivaled by even bigger creatures—the tyrannosaurs of the Cretaceous period.

Yanchuanosaurus

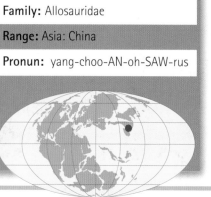

Ju Late Jurassic

Size: 33 ft/10 m long

Order: Saurischia

Family: Allosauridae

Range: Asia: China

Pronun: yang-choo-AN-oh-SAW-rus

Allosaurus

Yanchuanosaurus

Yangchuanosaurus had a huge head and powerful jaws. Its sharp fangs curved backward and had serated edges like steak knives. *Yangchuanosaurus* took all of its weight on its three clawed toes when it walked. It stayed balanced with its long tail, which made up about half of its total body length.

Allosaurus

This enormous dinosaur weighed 1–2 U.S. tons (1–2 tonnes), and must have stood some 15 ft (4.6 m) tall. Some scientists think it was too heavy and clumsy to have hunted, and instead fed on dead animals. Other paleontologists believe *Allosaurus* was very agile, and may even have hunted in packs to bring down giant, plant-eating dinosaurs.

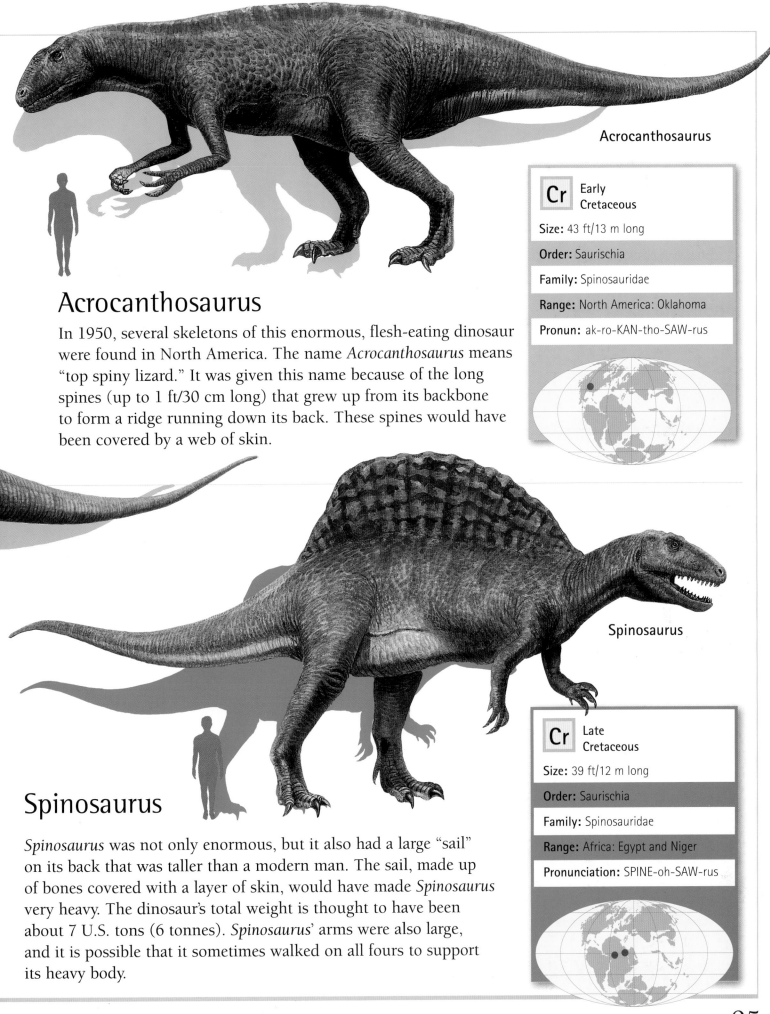

Acrocanthosaurus

In 1950, several skeletons of this enormous, flesh-eating dinosaur were found in North America. The name *Acrocanthosaurus* means "top spiny lizard." It was given this name because of the long spines (up to 1 ft/30 cm long) that grew up from its backbone to form a ridge running down its back. These spines would have been covered by a web of skin.

Acrocanthosaurus

Cr	Early Cretaceous
Size: 43 ft/13 m long	
Order: Saurischia	
Family: Spinosauridae	
Range: North America: Oklahoma	
Pronun: ak-ro-KAN-tho-SAW-rus	

Spinosaurus

Spinosaurus was not only enormous, but it also had a large "sail" on its back that was taller than a modern man. The sail, made up of bones covered with a layer of skin, would have made *Spinosaurus* very heavy. The dinosaur's total weight is thought to have been about 7 U.S. tons (6 tonnes). *Spinosaurus*' arms were also large, and it is possible that it sometimes walked on all fours to support its heavy body.

Spinosaurus

Cr	Late Cretaceous
Size: 39 ft/12 m long	
Order: Saurischia	
Family: Spinosauridae	
Range: Africa: Egypt and Niger	
Pronunciation: SPINE-oh-SAW-rus	

95

Tyrannosaurs

Alioramus

Tyrannosaurs, meaning "tyrant lizards," were the largest meat-eaters ever to have walked the Earth. These huge animals lived for only about 15 million years in the Late Cretaceous period, but they are among the most well-known of dinosaurs. They had large heads, sturdy legs, and tiny arms. Although tyrannosaurs are well known for their ferocious appearance, their size may have been a problem when hunting. Their bulky bodies made it hard to chase and catch prey. In reality, these big meat-eaters could have spent much of their time looking for dead animals to eat. However, they could have ambushed prey, attacking in short bursts of speed like a modern tiger.

Cr	Late Cretaceous

Size: 26 ft/8 m long

Order: Saurischia

Family: Tyrannosauridae

Range: North America: Alberta

Pronunciation: al-BERT-oh-SAW-rus

Albertosaurus

This creature had a big head and a short body. It was balanced by a long, strong tail and stood on pillar-like legs. Three toes spread out from each foot to support the dinosaur's great weight. *Albertosaurus*' arms were tiny compared to its body. They were so short that they could not have reached up to the mouth. There were only two fingers on each hand, which would not have been very effective for grasping prey.

Albertosaurus

Alioramus

Alioramus' head looked different from those of other tyrannosaurs. It had a flat skull with a long snout. It also had bony knobs or spikes on its face between the eyes and the tip of the snout. It lived in Asia and North America at a time when these modern continents were joined together to make one vast piece of land.

Cr	Late Cretaceous

Size: 20 ft/6 m long

Order: Saurischia

Family: Tyrannosauridae

Range: Asia: Mongolia

Pronunciation: ay-lee-oh-RAY-mus

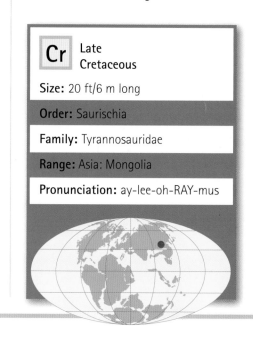

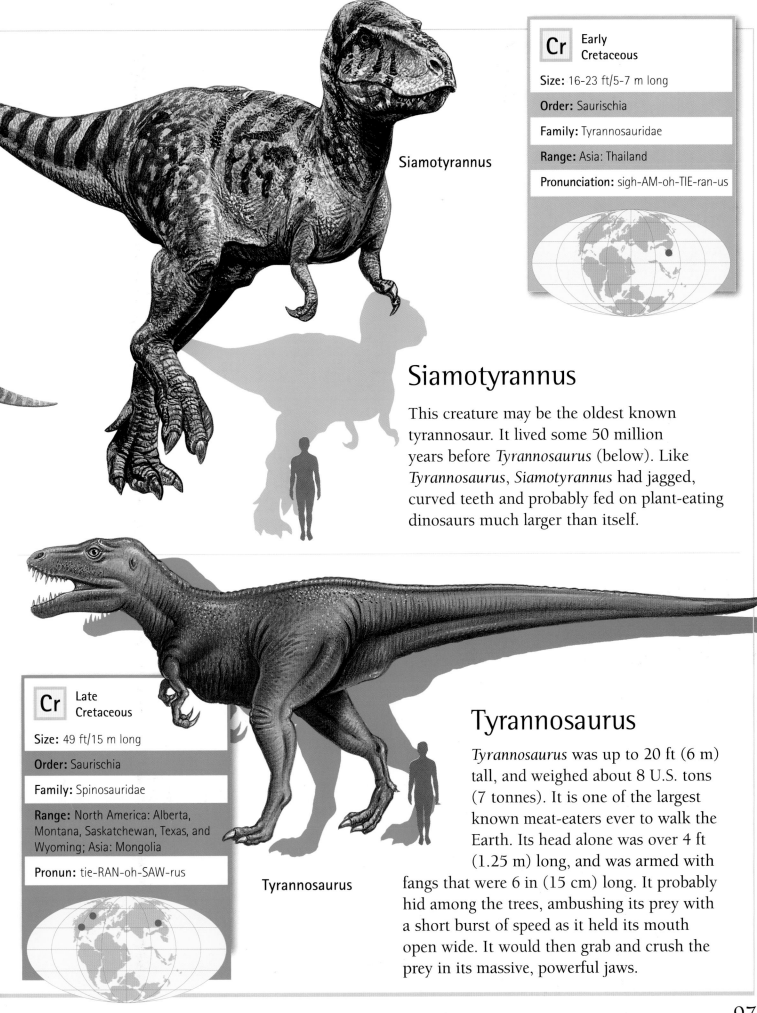

Siamotyrannus

Cr Early Cretaceous

Size: 16-23 ft/5-7 m long

Order: Saurischia

Family: Tyrannosauridae

Range: Asia: Thailand

Pronunciation: sigh-AM-oh-TIE-ran-us

Siamotyrannus

This creature may be the oldest known tyrannosaur. It lived some 50 million years before *Tyrannosaurus* (below). Like *Tyrannosaurus*, *Siamotyrannus* had jagged, curved teeth and probably fed on plant-eating dinosaurs much larger than itself.

Cr Late Cretaceous

Size: 49 ft/15 m long

Order: Saurischia

Family: Spinosauridae

Range: North America: Alberta, Montana, Saskatchewan, Texas, and Wyoming; Asia: Mongolia

Pronun: tie-RAN-oh-SAW-rus

Tyrannosaurus

Tyrannosaurus was up to 20 ft (6 m) tall, and weighed about 8 U.S. tons (7 tonnes). It is one of the largest known meat-eaters ever to walk the Earth. Its head alone was over 4 ft (1.25 m) long, and was armed with fangs that were 6 in (15 cm) long. It probably hid among the trees, ambushing its prey with a short burst of speed as it held its mouth open wide. It would then grab and crush the prey in its massive, powerful jaws.

Tyrannosaurus

Life in Jurassic Europe

T he Jurassic period lasted from 200 to 145 million years ago. It is named after the limestone that formed at this time in the sea and later became part of the European Jura Mountains. Changes in the climate brought about an explosion of new plant and animal life during the Jurassic period.

The dry deserts of the Triassic period mostly disappeared during early Jurassic times. The climate became much warmer and sea levels rose. Warm, sunlit waters on the coasts were good breeding grounds for marine life. By the end of the period, bony fish had developed that were similar to the fish we see today. They were hunted by the spectacular "sea monsters"—the ichthyosaurs and plesiosaurs of the Jurassic seas. On land, plants flourished in the warm, wet climate. Early mammals also thrived. Trees were large and lush, like the plants of today's tropical rainforests. The sky became busier as more flying reptiles (pterosaurs) emerged. By the end of the period, the first birds were beginning to appear.

Carnivorous Megalosaur: Megalosaurus

The first dinosaur bone ever discovered, found in England in 1676, probably belonged to *Megalosaurus*. With an overall length of 30 ft (9 m), a height of 10 ft (3 m), and a weight of 1 U.S. ton (900 kg), *Megalosaurus*, or "great lizard," was a massive creature. A short, strong neck carried its large head. Its powerful jaws were armed with curved, saw-edged fangs, and its strong fingers and toes had long claws. With such weapons, *Megalosaurus* was well-equipped to attack and kill large, long-necked plant-eating dinosaurs. *Megalosaurus* footprints can be seen in the rocks of southern England. They show how these bulky creatures walked on two legs. Their long tails probably swung from side to side at each step to balance the heavy body.

Herbivorous Sauropod: Cetiosaurus

Bones of this huge sauropod were discovered in 1809 in Southern England, 32 years before anyone had ever heard of "dinosaurs." People thought that the bones belonged to a great marine animal, which is why it is called *Cetiosaurus*, or "whale lizard." Others thought that the bones came from a huge crocodile. The dinosaur was massive, but it had a shorter neck than other sauropods. A skeleton of *Cetiosaurus* that was discovered in Morocco in 1979 helped paleontologists work out the size of the creature. The animal's thigh bone alone measured 6 ft (1.8 m) long. One of the shoulder blades was over 5 ft (1.5 m) long. *Cetiosaurus* may have weighed over 10 U.S. tons (9 tonnes). It would have had to eat an enormous amount of plant food to power its great limbs.

A giant hunter, *Megalosaurus*, stalks a *Cetiosaurus* and a herd of *Camptosaurus* during the Jurassic period.

Prosauropods

Plateosaurus

Prosauropods were herbivorous (plant-eating) dinosaurs that lived during Late Triassic times. The largest creatures in this group grew to over 30 ft (9 m) long. They walked on four legs and had long necks to reach up to the high branches of trees and bushes. Although prosauropods were four-legged herbivorous creatures, scientists believe they were related to two-legged meat-eating dinosaurs. The remains of two possible ancestors have been found in South America. *Staurikosaurus* lived around 215 million years ago and was about 6 ft 6 in (2 m) long. *Herrerasaurus* lived around 210 million years ago and was 10 ft (3 m) long. Both were fast-moving, two-legged flesh-eaters, with large heads and long tails.

Efraasia

Efraasia's body shape was typical of prosauropods. Its hands were useful for both walking and eating. Its long fingers could have grasped small plants and bundles of leaves with the help of its mobile "thumbs." The wrist was also very flexible. The palm of the hand could be pressed to the ground easily, so the animal could walk on all fours.

Tr	Late Triassic
Size: 8 ft/2.4 m long	
Order: Saurischia	
Family: Anchisauridae	
Range: Europe: Germany	
Pronunciation: e-FRAHS-ee-a	

Plateosaurus

Plateosaurus probably traveled in herds, looking for new feeding grounds. It was a large animal, with its tail making up about half its length. *Plateosaurus* would have moved about on all fours most of the time, occasionally standing up and stretching out its long neck to feed off higher branches.

Tr	Late Triassic
Size: 23 ft/7 m long	
Order: Saurischia	
Family: Plateosauridae	
Range: Europe: England, France, Germany and Switzerland	
Pronunciation: PLAT-ee-oh-SAW-rus	

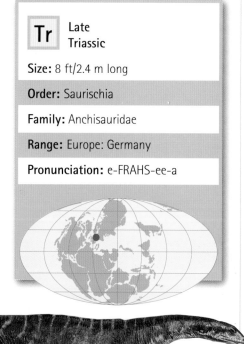
Efraasia

Anchisaurus

Anchisaurus was a small, lightly-built prosauropod. It had a small head, tall, flexible neck, and long, slim body. Its arms were shorter than its legs, and it probably moved about on two legs as well as four. Each hand had five fingers, but the two on the outer most side were very short. The first finger, or "thumb," had a large, sharp claw, which may have been used for digging up plants or for fighting.

Ju	Early Jurassic

Size: 7 ft/2.1 m long

Order: Saurischia

Family: Anchisauridae

Range: North America: Arizona and Connecticut; southern Africa

Pronunciation: AN-ki-SAW-rus

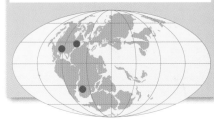

Anchisaurus

Mussaurus

When paleontologists found some tiny dinosaur bones in Argentina in 1979, they thought they had discovered the smallest ever dinosaur. They called it *Mussaurus*—"mouse lizard." However, experts now think that these skeletons were of young animals, as there were two fossilized eggs nearby. An adult *Mussaurus* could have grown up to 10 ft (3 m) long.

Mussaurus

Tr–Ju	Late Triassic to Early Jurassic

Size: 10 ft/3 m long

Order: Saurischia

Family: Plateosauridae

Range: South America: Argentina

Pronunciation: moo-SAW-rus

Sauropods

Between 65 and 200 million years ago, the largest plant-eaters were the giant long-necked, four-legged sauropods. In fact, these dinosaurs were the largest animals ever to have lived on land. They became extinct by the end of the Cretaceous period. Most sauropods were huge—well over 50 ft (15 m) long. Each had a small head on top of an extra-long neck. The body was very deep to hold an enormous stomach. Thick, pillar-like legs with five-toed feet supported its great weight. A long, thick tail was used for balance when walking.

Ju	Late Jurassic
Size: 75 ft/23 m long	
Order: Saurischia	
Family: Brachiosauridae	
Range: North America: Colorado; Africa: Tanzania and Algeria	
Pronunciation: BRAK-ee-oh-SAW-rus	

Brachiosaurus

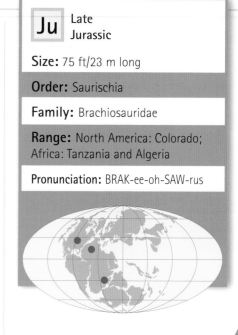

Barapasaurus

Ju	Early Jurassic
Size: 49 ft/15 m long	
Order: Saurischia	
Family: Barapasauridae	
Range: Asia: India	
Pronunciation: ba-RA-pa-SAW-rus	

Barapasaurus, found in India, is the world's oldest known sauropod. It was built like other sauropods, but some of the bones in its neck and back were hollow to make its body lighter. *Barapasaurus'* teeth were spoon-shaped and saw-edged, ideal for eating plants.

Brachiosaurus

A complete skeleton of *Brachiosaurus* was discovered during an expedition in 1908–12. It is the largest complete skeleton in existence. *Brachiosaurus* was about 41 ft (12.6 m) tall. Its shoulders were 21 ft (6.4 m) off the ground. It weighed an enormous 89 U.S. tons (80 tonnes)—the same weight as 12 modern adult African bull elephants.

Barapasaurus

Camarasaurus

Ju Late Jurassic

Size: 59 ft/18 m long

Order: Saurischia

Family: Camarasauridae

Range: North America: Colorado, Oklahoma, Utah, and Wyoming

Pronunciation: kam-AR-a-SAW-rus

This creature probably roamed in herds for great distances looking for food. It lived on the tropical plains that covered western North America during the Jurassic period. Its heavy, spoon-shaped teeth were good for eating tough plants, such as ferns and horsetails. It could have reached up to the high branches of conifer trees, tearing away great mouthfuls of needle-like leaves.

Camarasaurus

Opisthocoelicaudia

Only one skeleton of *Opisthocoelicaudia* has been found. As this is missing its neck and head, paleontologists are not sure what *Opisthocoelicaudia* looked like, or how big it was. The rest of its body is typical of a sauropod. *Opisthocoelicaudia* had a very large, thick tail. Paleontologists think that the tail was used to prop the animal up when it reared up on back legs to feed on the high branches of trees.

Opisthocoelicaudia

Cr Late Cretaceous

Size: 40 ft/12.2 m long

Order: Saurischia

Family: Camarasauridae

Range: Asia: Mongolia

Pronun: oh-PIS-tho-SEEL-i-CAWD-ee-a

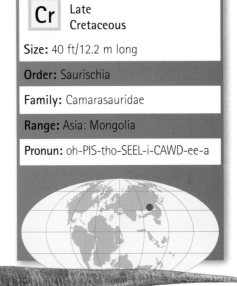

Ju Late Jurassic

Size: 85 ft/26 m long

Order: Saurischia

Family: Diplodocidae

Range: North America: Colorado, Montana, Utah, and Wyoming

Pronunciation: di-PLOD-oh-cus

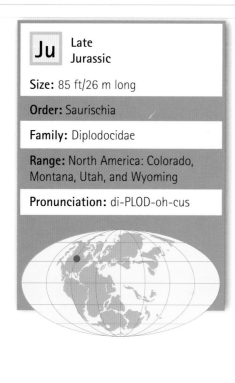

Apatosaurus

This giant, plant-eating dinosaur was once know as *Brontosaurus*, which means "thunder lizard." This refers to the noise this 33 U.S. ton (30 tonne) animal would have made when it walked. *Apatosaurus*' total body length was over 65 ft (20 m), but its tiny head was only 22 in (55 cm) long. Its great weight could have been used to ward off attack—it could have reared up and then brought its heavy front legs down to crush its enemy.

Ju Late Jurassic

Size: 70 ft/21.3 m long

Order: Saurischia

Family: Diplodocidae

Range: North America: Colorado, Oklahoma, Utah, and Wyoming

Pronunciation: a-PAT-oh-SAW-rus

Apatosaurus

Diplodocus

Diplodocus was a huge animal. Some of them reached lengths of 100 ft (30 m). Most of its length was taken up by the long neck (about 24 ft/7.3 m), and the extra-long tail (about 46 ft/14 m). The body was only about 13 ft (4 m) long, and the tiny head measured just over 2 ft (60 cm) in length. *Diplodocus* had very hollow bones, so despite its great size, it weighed only 11 U.S. tons (10 tonnes).

Diplodocus

104

Mamenchisaurus

This animal had the longest neck of any known dinosaur. As the animal walked, its stiff neck must have been held out almost straight in front of its body. This super-long neck meant *Mamenchisaurus* was able to reach the freshest leaves at the very tips of the highest branches of conifer trees.

Ju	Late Jurassic
Size: 72 ft/22 m long	
Order: Saurischia	
Family: Diplodocidae	
Range: Asia: Mongolia	
Pronun: mah-MUHN-chee-SAW-rus	

Saltasaurus

Saltasaurus had bony plates all over its back and sides. Most of these were tiny, about ¼ in (5 mm) across, but others were larger, about 4½ in (11 cm) across, and could have had spikes. These plates would have made a kind of armor to protect *Saltasaurus* against flesh-eating dinosaurs. These armored sauropods have been found mainly in South America.

Cr	Late Cretaceous
Size: 39 ft/12 m long	
Order: Saurischia	
Family: Titanosauridae	
Range: South America: Argentina	
Pronunciation: SALT-a-SAW-rus	

Saltasaurus

Life in Cretaceous Mongolia

The remote deserts of Mongolia have produced some amazing fossils. In Cretaceous times, the area was swept by dust storms that buried the remains of hundreds of animals. Even the smallest, most delicate bones were preserved. They provide a window into life on Earth around 90 million years ago.

One of the most famous dinosaur fossils found in Mongolia is that of *Oviraptor*, or "egg stealer." It was given this name when its remains were found with a nest of eggs that scientists thought belonged to another Cretaceous dinosaur called *Protoceratops*. It was thought that *Oviraptor* fed on *Protoceratops'* eggs. Scientists now know, however, that these fossilized eggs contained embryos that belonged to *Oviraptor*. The "egg stealer" actually died sitting on its own nest.

Birdlike Dinosaur: Gallimimus

Gallimimus was one of the largest known ornithomimids, or birdlike dinosaurs. It had a long snout with a wide, flat beak. Its hands were shaped like spades, which would have made it difficult for the dinosaur to grasp food. It may have used its hands to dig up other dinosaurs' eggs to eat. In 1965, a much larger birdlike dinosaur, called *Deinocheirus*, was found in the Gobi Desert in Mongolia. It had arms measuring 8 ft (2.5 m) from the shoulder to the tip of the three powerful, clawed fingers. Each claw bone was about 10 in (25 cm). No other parts of the skeleton have been found, so it is impossible to say to what family this dinosaur belonged.

Protoceratops

Velociraptor

Protoceratops

Oviraptor

Kennalestes

Carnivorous Tyrannosaur: Tarbosaurus

This giant carnosaur lumbered around eating anything it came across, dead or alive. Its huge size meant that it probably wasn't quick enough to be a great hunter. It would have preyed on the large plant-eating dinosaurs and also eaten meat left by other carnosaurs. Many *Tarbosaurus* skeletons have been discovered in Mongolia. Its skeleton is almost the same as that of *Tyrannosaurus*, but *Tarbosaurus* was lighter and had a longer skull. Its back was held very straight and its body was balanced on its hips. Its long neck was very flexible and its tail stretched out behind to keep *Tarbosaurus* balanced when walking.

Although dinosaurs ruled the Cretaceous period, small mammals were becoming more numerous. Like mammals today, most Cretaceous mammals gave birth to well-developed young. Then, as now, marsupials gave birth to helpless young that continued to grow in the mother's pouch. Monotremes were egg-laying mammals, like the modern Australian platypus.

Below: Plant-eaters such as *Oviraptor* and *Gallimimus* were hunted through the desert by fierce predators such as *Velociraptor* and *Tarbosaurus*. *Protoceratops* laid eggs on the ground in mud-mound nests. Small mammals, such as *Zalambdalestes*, *Kennalestes*, and *Kamptobaatar*, were also common.

Gallimimus

Tarbosaurus

Mononykus

Zalambdalestes

Kamptobaatar

Fabrosaurs and Heterodonts

The ornithopods, or "bird feet," were a very successful group of dinosaurs. They survived for 148 million years throughout the Jurassic and Cretaceous periods. Fabrosaurs and heterodonts both belonged to this group. Fabrosaurs are the earliest known ornithopods and date back some 200 million years. They were small, lizard-like animals, but they ran upright on two long, slender legs. Heterodonts were among the first dinosaurs to develop cheeks, which stopped food from falling out of their mouths while they chewed.

Ju/Cr	Late Jurassic or Early Cretaceous
Size: 2 ft/60 cm long	
Order: Ornithischia	
Family: Fabrosauridae	
Range: Europe: England	
Pronunciation: e-KIEN-o-don	

Echinodon

Lesothosaurus

Ju	Early Jurassic
Size: 3 ft 3 in/1 m long	
Order: Ornithischia	
Family: Fabrosauridae	
Range: Africa: Lesotho	
Pronunciation: less-OH-toe-SAW-rus	

This small animal was lightly built and a fast runner. It had long legs, short arms, and a slender tail. Its pointed teeth had grooved edges that could have chopped up tough plants. Once worn, these teeth may have fallen out and been replaced by new ones.

Echinodon

Only the jaw bones of this small creature have been found, but these show that *Echinodon* had unusual teeth. Most reptiles' teeth are all the same size and shape. *Echinodon*, however, had long, sharp canine teeth at the front of its jaws. Similar teeth were also found in the heterodonts.

Lesothosaurus

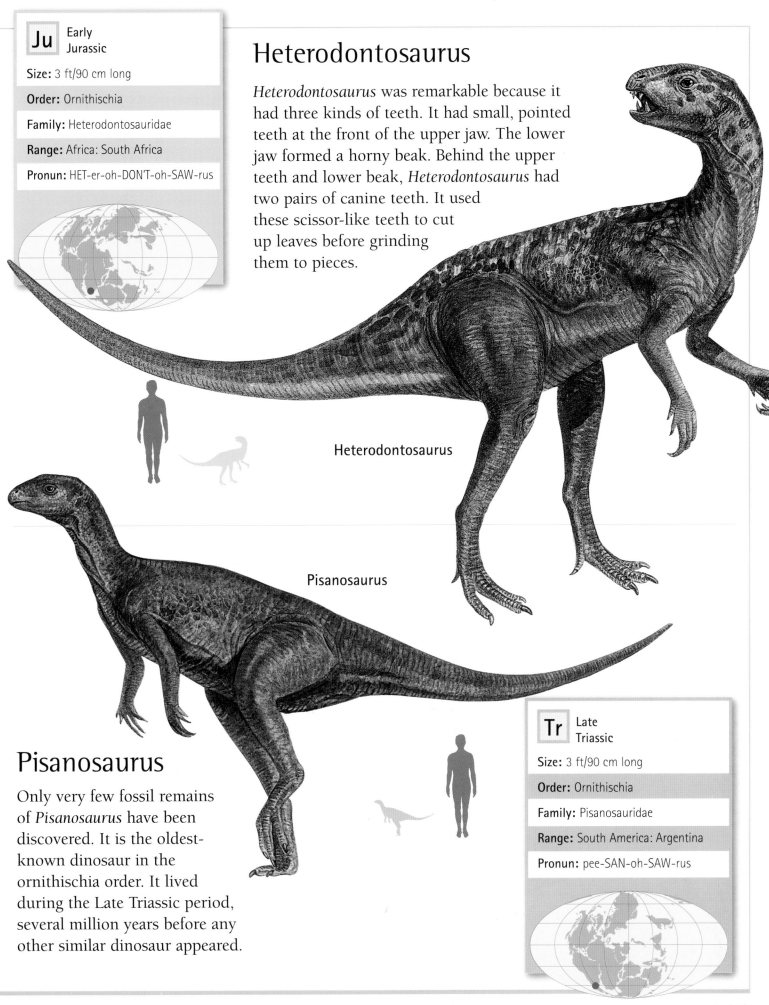

Ju	Early Jurassic
Size: 3 ft/90 cm long	
Order: Ornithischia	
Family: Heterodontosauridae	
Range: Africa: South Africa	
Pronun: HET-er-oh-DON'T-oh-SAW-rus	

Heterodontosaurus

Heterodontosaurus was remarkable because it had three kinds of teeth. It had small, pointed teeth at the front of the upper jaw. The lower jaw formed a horny beak. Behind the upper teeth and lower beak, *Heterodontosaurus* had two pairs of canine teeth. It used these scissor-like teeth to cut up leaves before grinding them to pieces.

Heterodontosaurus

Pisanosaurus

Pisanosaurus

Only very few fossil remains of *Pisanosaurus* have been discovered. It is the oldest-known dinosaur in the ornithischia order. It lived during the Late Triassic period, several million years before any other similar dinosaur appeared.

Tr	Late Triassic
Size: 3 ft/90 cm long	
Order: Ornithischia	
Family: Pisanosauridae	
Range: South America: Argentina	
Pronun: pee-SAN-oh-SAW-rus	

109

Boneheads

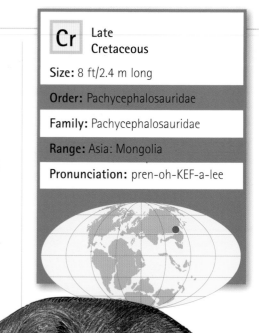

Cr Late Cretaceous

Size: 8 ft/2.4 m long

Order: Pachycephalosauridae

Family: Pachycephalosauridae

Range: Asia: Mongolia

Pronunciation: pren-oh-KEF-a-lee

Boneheads were very strange-looking dinosaurs. Their scientific name, pachycephalosaur, means "thick-headed lizard" and refers to their high foreheads and dome-shaped skull caps made up of enormous, thickened bone. Some species also had bony frills, knobs, and spikes on the backs and sides of their heads, and sometimes on their snouts. Many paleontologists believe that these boneheaded dinosaurs lived together in herds like modern mountain goats. Males would have fought in head-butting contests to see who would lead the herd and mate with females. Like ornithopods, they walked on two feet and fed on plants.

Prenocephale

Cr Late Cretaceous

Size: 6 ft 6 in/2 m long

Order: Ornithischia

Family: Pachycephalosauridae

Range: North America: Alberta

Pronunciation: steg-O-ser-as

Stegoceras

When *Stegoceras* charged at a rival, it would have lowered its head and held its neck, body, and tail stiff for balance. The skull cap was a dome of solid bone, and the small brain was well protected inside. A full-grown *Stegoceras* could have weighed 120 lb (55 kg).

Prenocephale

Prenocephale had a row of bony spikes and bumps around the back and sides of its solid skull. The females probably had smaller, thinner skulls than the males. Like other boneheaded dinosaurs, *Prenocephale* probably had large eyes and a very good sense of smell. It lived in forests where it fed on leaves and fruits.

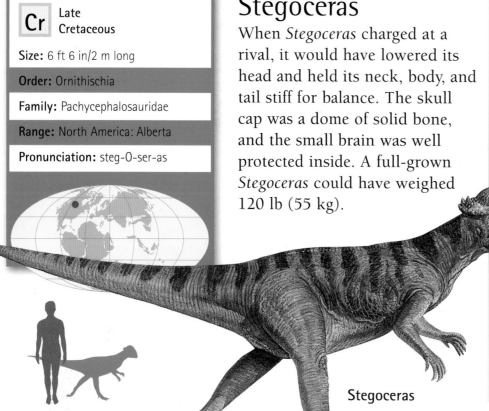

Stegoceras

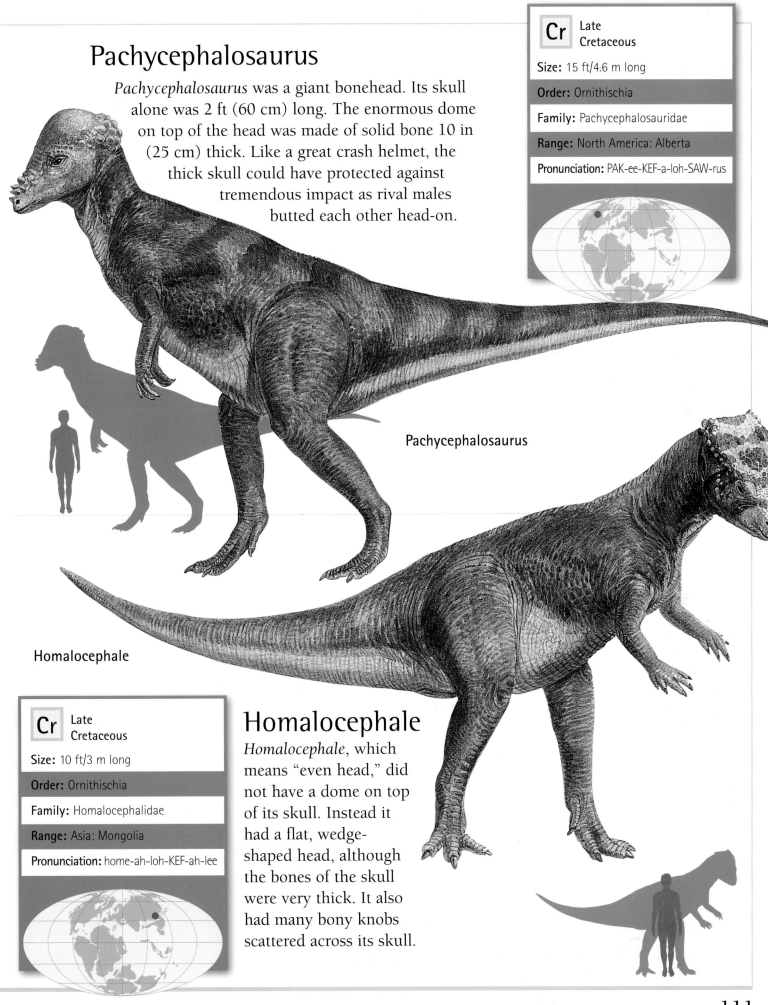

Pachycephalosaurus

Pachycephalosaurus was a giant bonehead. Its skull alone was 2 ft (60 cm) long. The enormous dome on top of the head was made of solid bone 10 in (25 cm) thick. Like a great crash helmet, the thick skull could have protected against tremendous impact as rival males butted each other head-on.

Cr Late Cretaceous

Size: 15 ft/4.6 m long

Order: Ornithischia

Family: Pachycephalosauridae

Range: North America: Alberta

Pronunciation: PAK-ee-KEF-a-loh-SAW-rus

Pachycephalosaurus

Homalocephale

Cr Late Cretaceous

Size: 10 ft/3 m long

Order: Ornithischia

Family: Homalocephalidae

Range: Asia: Mongolia

Pronunciation: home-ah-loh-KEF-ah-lee

Homalocephale

Homalocephale, which means "even head," did not have a dome on top of its skull. Instead it had a flat, wedge-shaped head, although the bones of the skull were very thick. It also had many bony knobs scattered across its skull.

Life in Cretaceous Belgium

One of the world's most exciting fossil finds was made in Belgium in 1878. While working in a pit, two coal miners found complete skeletons of large plant-eating dinosaurs. The skeletons all belonged to *Iguanodon*.

Iguanodon was a large dinosaur that weighed about 2 U.S. tons (1.9 tonnes). Its hip bones and hind legs were birdlike, but unlike birds, it had a long muscular tail and strong arms, wrists, and hands. Young *Iguanodons* probably stood on two legs, but heavier adults would have walked on four legs. *Iguanodon* had powerful jaws, strong cheek teeth, and a horny beak that could break down the tough plant foods it ate, including horsetails and conifers.

The plant-eating *Hypsilophodon* was also found in Belgium in the Cretaceous period. *Hypsilophodon* was built for speed and agility. It could run fast and turn quickly like a modern gazelle. Another herbivore was the four-legged *Polacanthus*, which had an armored body for defence against meat-eating predators, like *Megalosaurus*.

In the Cretaceous period England was joined to what is now mainland Europe. A vast floodplain covered the area between Belgium and southern England. *Iguanodon* and other plant-eating dinosaurs survived on the horsetails that grew in the water-logged land. The herbivorous dinosaurs were preyed upon by carnosaurs such as *Megalosaurus*. *Baryonyx* and *Bernissartia* fed on fish such as *Lepidotes*.

Polacanthus

Megalosaurus

Baryonyx

Hypsilophodon

Lepidotes

Cretaceous Crocodile: Bernissartia

Bernissartia lived along the shores of the shallow Wealden Lake, which stretched from southeast England into Belgium. It thrived during the Early Cretaceous period, some 130 million years ago. *Bernissartia* led a semi-aquatic life— spending some of its time in the water and some on land. It had two types of teeth in its jaws. Those at the front were long and pointed, and were good for catching fish. Those at the back were broad and flat. These would be used for crushing shellfish or the bones of dead animals.

Carnivorous Dinosaur: Baryonyx

Baryonyx had two unusual features. First, it had two huge, curved claws, about 1 ft (30 cm) long, which were probably attached to its front feet. Secondly, *Baryonyx*'s skull was long and narrow, rather like that of a crocodile, and the dinosaur had twice as many small, pointed teeth as any of its relatives. Paleontologists think that *Baryonyx* hunted on all fours along river banks, hooking fish out of the water with its long claws. This is similar to the way grizzly bears fish along river banks today.

Tree ferns

Iguanodon

Baryonyx

Bernissartia

Horsetails

Hypsilophodonts

Hypsilophodonts were among the most successful dinosaurs. They lived for about 100 million years, from the Late Jurassic to the end of the Cretaceous period, and spread to every continent in the world except Asia. Hypsilophodonts were herbivorous animals. They had cheeks to stop food from falling out of their mouths and teeth that were designed for chewing and grinding tough plants. Like modern gazelles, these dinosaurs probably lived in herds and would have always been alert to predators. When danger threatened, their lightweight bodies and long legs meant that they could sprint away at high speed.

Parksosaurus

Similar to all other hypsilophodonts, *Parksosaurus* had short arms, long shins, and feet for sprinting. A stiff tail helped it balance. It had a small head with a horny beak instead of front teeth and large eyes. *Parksosaurus* probably looked for its food close to the ground, snuffling about among low-growing plants. It would nip off bits of plant food with its narrow, beaked jaws.

Cr	Early Cretaceous
Size: 5 ft/1.5 m long	
Order: Ornithischia	
Family: Hypsilophodontidae	
Range: North America: South Dakota; Europe: England and Portugal	
Pronunciation: hip-see-LOAF-oh-don	

Hypsilophodon

Hypsilophodon is the classic representative of the hypsilophodont family. Its name means "high ridge tooth," and refers to the tall, grooved cheek teeth that are a typical feature of all hypsilophodonts. Its upper and lower teeth met in regular rows rather than interlocking. This formed a flat surface that was perfect for grinding up tough plants.

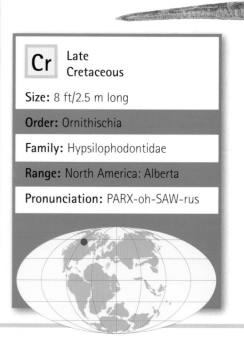

Cr	Late Cretaceous
Size: 8 ft/2.5 m long	
Order: Ornithischia	
Family: Hypsilophodontidae	
Range: North America: Alberta	
Pronunciation: PARX-oh-SAW-rus	

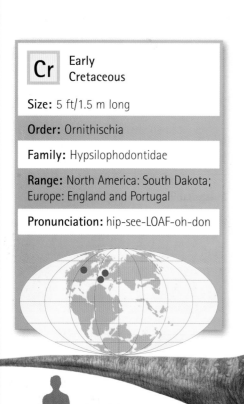

Hypsilophodon

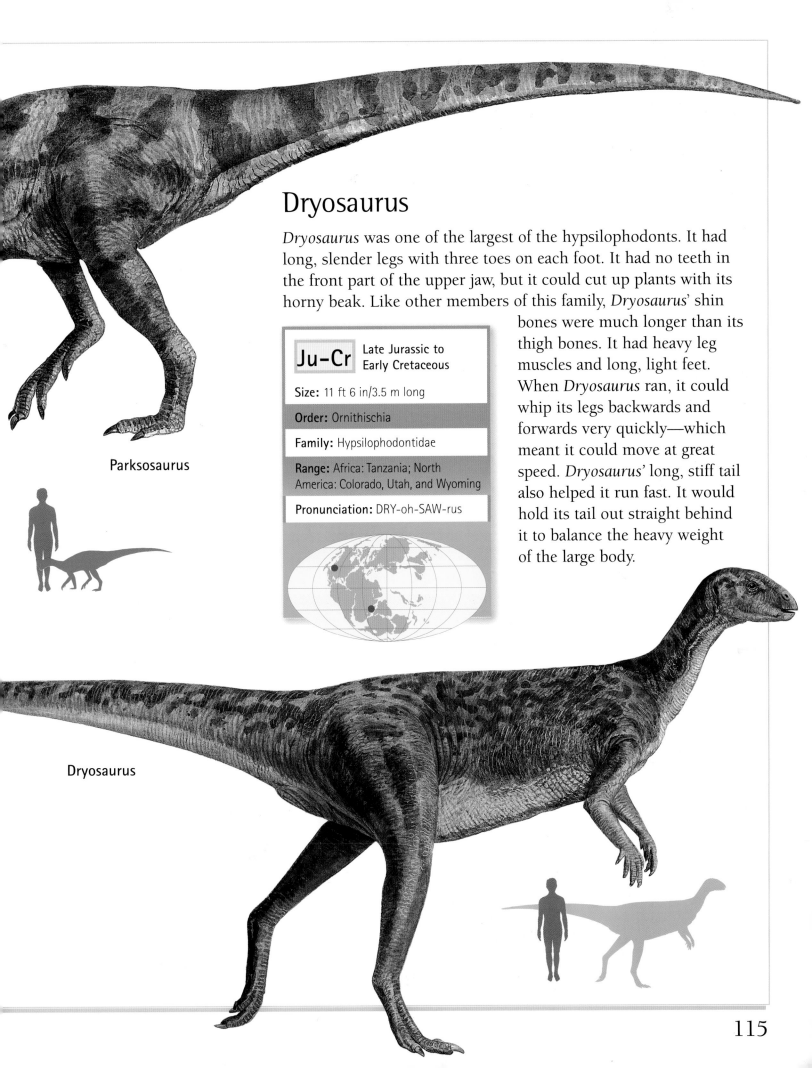

Dryosaurus

Dryosaurus was one of the largest of the hypsilophodonts. It had long, slender legs with three toes on each foot. It had no teeth in the front part of the upper jaw, but it could cut up plants with its horny beak. Like other members of this family, *Dryosaurus'* shin bones were much longer than its thigh bones. It had heavy leg muscles and long, light feet. When *Dryosaurus* ran, it could whip its legs backwards and forwards very quickly—which meant it could move at great speed. *Dryosaurus'* long, stiff tail also helped it run fast. It would hold its tail out straight behind it to balance the heavy weight of the large body.

Parksosaurus

Ju-Cr	Late Jurassic to Early Cretaceous

Size: 11 ft 6 in/3.5 m long

Order: Ornithischia

Family: Hypsilophodontidae

Range: Africa: Tanzania; North America: Colorado, Utah, and Wyoming

Pronunciation: DRY-oh-SAW-rus

Dryosaurus

115

Tenontosaurus

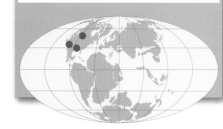
Othnielia

Othnielia was a typical hypsilophodont. It had long legs and a long tail, a lightweight body, and short arms with five-fingered hands. Only its teeth were different. They were smaller than those of other hypsilophodonts and had protective tooth enamel all over the surface, not just on the grinding edge. It is possible that *Othnielia* ate tougher plants and the enamel prevented its teeth from getting worn down.

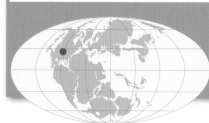
Tenontosaurus

This dinosaur was much larger than other hypsilophodonts. Over half the total length of *Tenontosaurus* was made up of the tail, which was enormously thick and heavy. The animal probably weighed about 1 U.S. ton (900 kg). It had longer arms than other hypsilophodonts and probably spent much of its time walking about on all-fours.

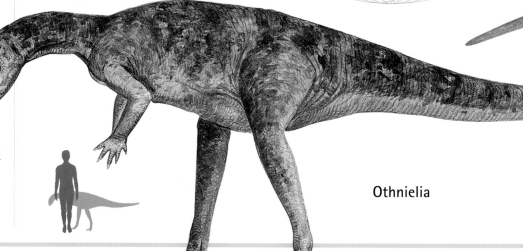

Othnielia

Thescelosaurus

Thescelosaurus was different from other hypsilophodonts in several ways. It had teeth in the front of its upper jaw, and five rather than three or four toes on each foot. It was bulky and big boned, and its thigh bones were as long as its shin bones. The shape of its legs might mean that *Thescelosaurus* was not a gazelle-type sprinter, but a slower-moving creature.

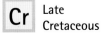

Thescelosaurus

Leaellynasaura

Fossils of this dinosaur were found in 1987 in the south of Australia. In the Early Cretaceous period, this region had a climate like that of the freezing North or South poles. *Leaellynasaura* must have been able to survive the long dark winters and icy cold temperatures. Its eye sockets were unusually large, suggesting that it had excellent sight.

Leaellynasaura

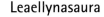

Living in a Herd

I t is impossible to be sure how dinosaurs lived, but evidence such as fossilized footprints can provide valuable clues. Groups of footprints have been discovered, for example, that suggest that dinosaurs moved in herds, just like many plant-eating animals today. Smaller footprints in among the big ones may have belonged to young dinosaurs. They would walk in the center of the herd for protection from predators.

Fossilized Footprints

Long ago, a herd of large dinosaurs would come to rivers to drink, leaving their footprints in the mud. Long dry spells would follow and the footprints were baked hard. Even though they were later covered by more mud, the prints remained. Millions of years later, as the surface of the land is worn away, the footprints are once again revealed, telling their story about the lives of dinosaurs.

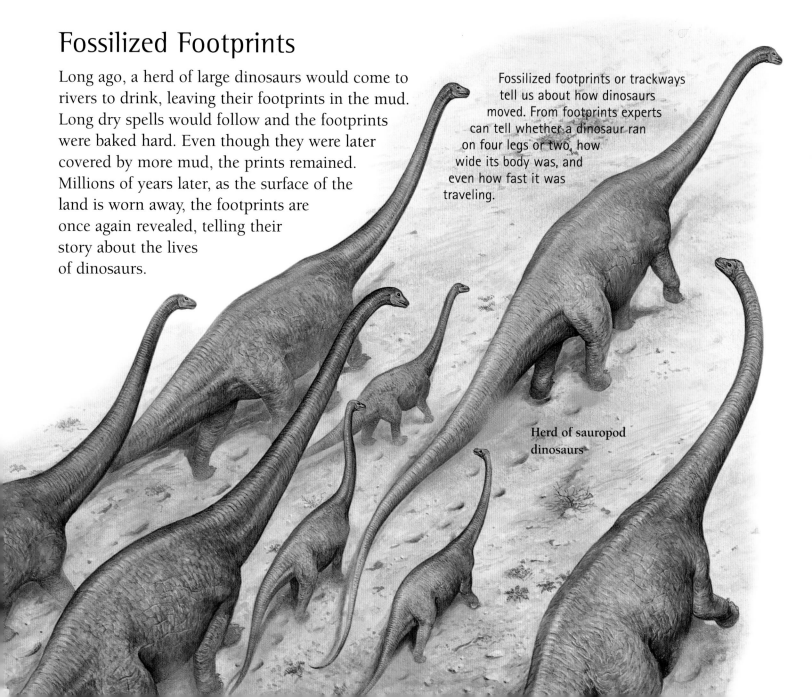

Fossilized footprints or trackways tell us about how dinosaurs moved. From footprints experts can tell whether a dinosaur ran on four legs or two, how wide its body was, and even how fast it was traveling.

Herd of sauropod dinosaurs

Camarasaurus

Parents and Young

Young dinosaurs, even the young of large sauropod dinosaurs like *Camarasaurus*, would have been vulnerable to attack by predators. For safety they would have stayed near their parents and moved at the center of the herd. The fossilized bones of young sauropods show that they grew very quickly. They may have gained as much as 7 lb (3 kg) in weight every day.

Horned Dinosaurs

Horned dinosaurs such as *Triceratops* are thought to have lived in herds. Just like herds of musk oxen today, they may have defended their young against attack by forming a circle around them and threatening the predator with their mighty horned heads.

Iguanodonts

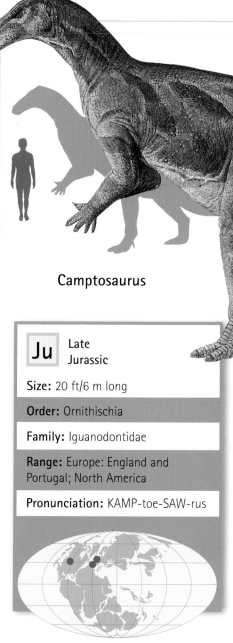

Camptosaurus

The iguanodonts emerged in the Mid Jurassic period about 170 million years ago. They spread throughout the world and thrived until the end of the Cretaceous period. Iguanodonts were large plant-eating dinosaurs. Their bodies were bulky and big-boned, and they had heavy, hooflike nails on both their front and back feet. They were probably slow-moving creatures that spent most of their time on all four legs, eating low-growing plants. Their beaklike jaws would nip off the leaves, and the rows of ridged cheek teeth would then grind them down to a pulp. These dinosaurs could also rear up on their hind legs to reach higher vegetation and to escape from predators.

Ju	Late Jurassic
Size: 20 ft/6 m long	
Order: Ornithischia	
Family: Iguanodontidae	
Range: Europe: England and Portugal; North America	
Pronunciation: KAMP-toe-SAW-rus	

Ju	Middle Jurassic
Size: 11 ft 6 in/3.5 m long	
Order: Ornithischia	
Family: Iguanodontidae	
Range: Europe: England	
Pronunciation: ka-LOH-vo-SAW-rus	

Callovosaurus

Callovosaurus is the earliest-known member of the iguanodonts. Only a single thigh bone has been found of this dinosaur, but paleontologists think that it looked a lot like the later dinosaur *Camptosaurus* (right).

Camptosaurus

Camptosaurus had a wide, heavy skull. Its snout was long and the jaws formed a toothless beak at the tip. A bony plate separated the breathing passages and the eating areas in its mouth, which meant that *Camptosaurus* could breathe and chew at the same time. This was important because *Camptosaurus* had to spend most of its time eating to get enough energy for its large body.

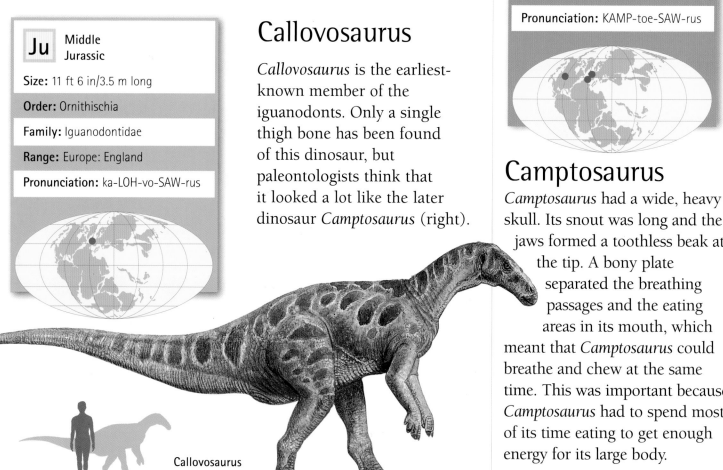

Callovosaurus

Iguanodon

Iguanodon was the second of all dinosaurs to be discovered, in 1809. It probably weighed about 5 U.S. tons (4.5 tonnes). Herds of *Iguanodon* would have roamed around, eating ferns and horsetails near rivers. Although they usually walked on all-fours, they could also walk upright, using their long tails for balance. The legs were long, and each arm had a five-fingered hand. The "thumb" of each hand was formed into a spike. The spikes could have been used to tear down plants, or as defense against attacks from predators.

Iguanodon

Cr Early Cretaceous
Size: 30 ft/9 m long
Order: Ornithischia
Family: Iguanodontidae
Range: Europe: Belgium, England, and Germany; North America: Utah; Africa: Tunisia; Asia: Mongolia
Pronunciation: ig-WA-no-don

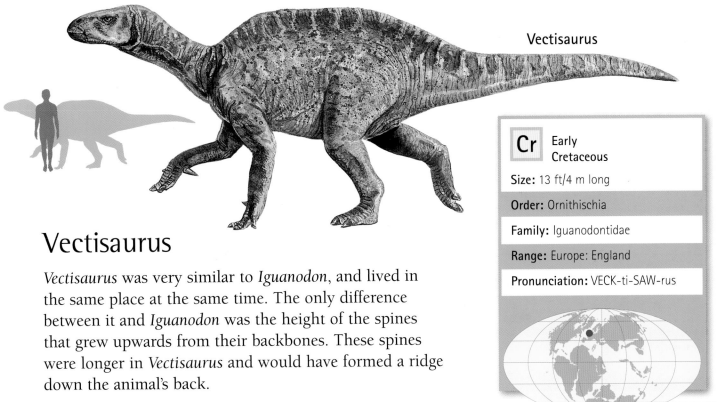

Vectisaurus

Cr Early Cretaceous
Size: 13 ft/4 m long
Order: Ornithischia
Family: Iguanodontidae
Range: Europe: England
Pronunciation: VECK-ti-SAW-rus

Vectisaurus

Vectisaurus was very similar to *Iguanodon*, and lived in the same place at the same time. The only difference between it and *Iguanodon* was the height of the spines that grew upwards from their backbones. These spines were longer in *Vectisaurus* and would have formed a ridge down the animal's back.

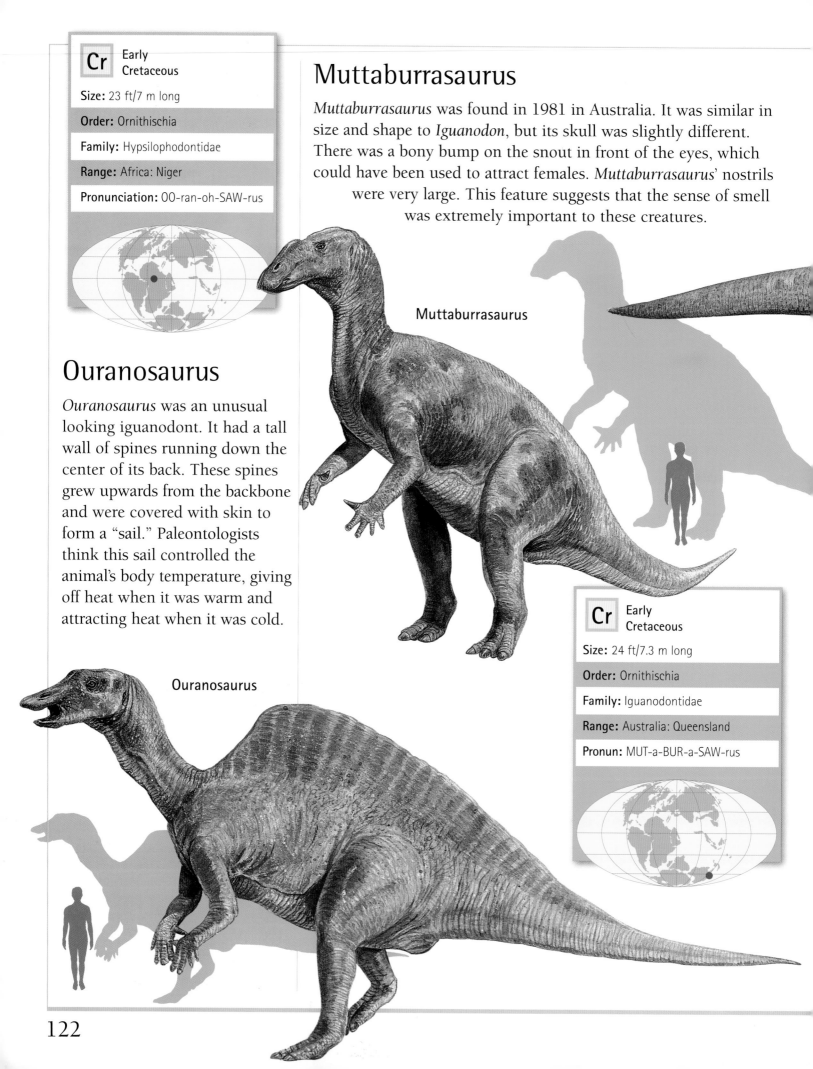

Cr	Early Cretaceous
Size: 23 ft/7 m long	
Order: Ornithischia	
Family: Hypsilophodontidae	
Range: Africa: Niger	
Pronunciation: OO-ran-oh-SAW-rus	

Muttaburrasaurus

Muttaburrasaurus was found in 1981 in Australia. It was similar in size and shape to *Iguanodon*, but its skull was slightly different. There was a bony bump on the snout in front of the eyes, which could have been used to attract females. *Muttaburrasaurus*' nostrils were very large. This feature suggests that the sense of smell was extremely important to these creatures.

Muttaburrasaurus

Ouranosaurus

Ouranosaurus was an unusual looking iguanodont. It had a tall wall of spines running down the center of its back. These spines grew upwards from the backbone and were covered with skin to form a "sail." Paleontologists think this sail controlled the animal's body temperature, giving off heat when it was warm and attracting heat when it was cold.

Ouranosaurus

Cr	Early Cretaceous
Size: 24 ft/7.3 m long	
Order: Ornithischia	
Family: Iguanodontidae	
Range: Australia: Queensland	
Pronun: MUT-a-BUR-a-SAW-rus	

Probactrosaurus

Probactrosaurus was one of the few iguanodonts to survive to the end of the Mesozoic era. It had a strong toothless beak for chopping up mouthfuls of plant food. It moved both on its two back legs and on all four legs.

Cr Early Cretaceous

Size: 20 ft/6 m long

Order: Ornithischia

Family: Iguanodontidae

Range: Asia: China

Pronun: pro-BAK-troh-SAW-rus

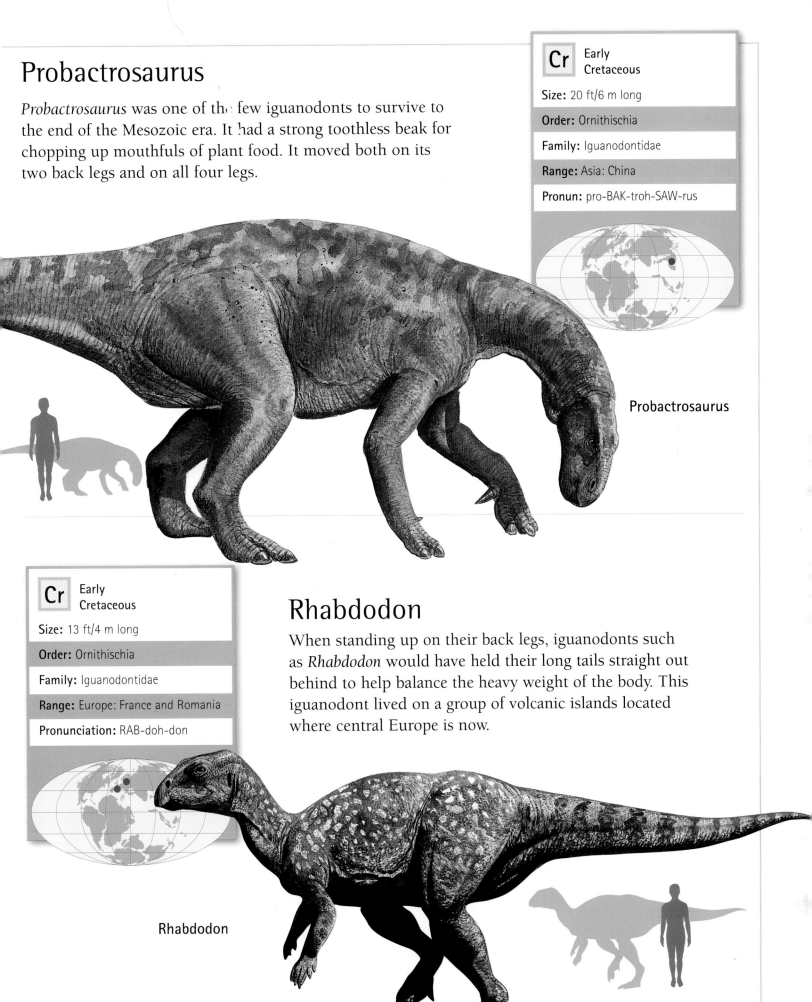

Probactrosaurus

Cr Early Cretaceous

Size: 13 ft/4 m long

Order: Ornithischia

Family: Iguanodontidae

Range: Europe: France and Romania

Pronunciation: RAB-doh-don

Rhabdodon

When standing up on their back legs, iguanodonts such as *Rhabdodon* would have held their long tails straight out behind to help balance the heavy weight of the body. This iguanodont lived on a group of volcanic islands located where central Europe is now.

Rhabdodon

123

Life in Cretaceous Alberta

More than 300 dinosaur skeletons have been found along the Red Deer River in Alberta, Canada. They date from the Cretaceous period, around 75 million years ago. No other rocky place on Earth has produced so many different dinosaur fossils.

By studying the earth and the many fossils found in Alberta, Canada, paleontologists know that there were a variety of environments in the area during the Cretaceous period. Animals lived in lagoons, swamps, rivers, and on the shores. Scientists have found 36 species of dinosaur and 84 species of fish, amphibian, reptile, bird, and mammal. There was plenty of water, which meant that lush plants and trees could grow. Plant-eating duckbilled dinosaurs like *Maiasaura* and *Parasaurolophus* flourished. They lived in herds and fed off the rich plant life. At the same time, larger, meat-eating dinosaurs roamed the land, hunting or feeding on dead animals.

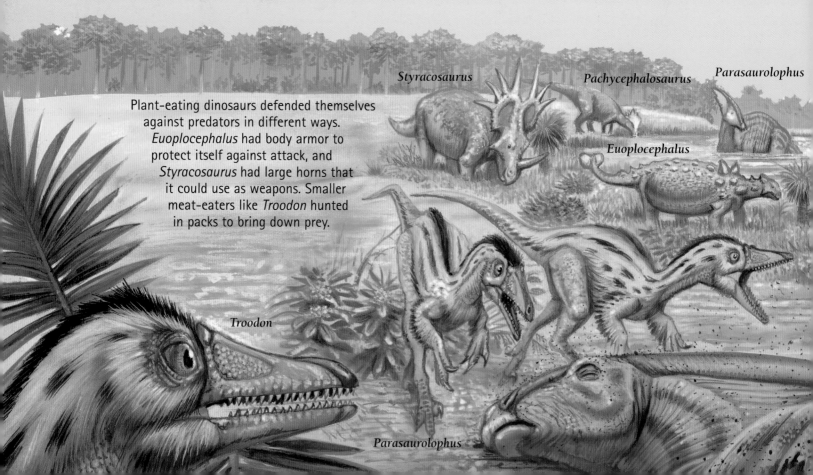

Plant-eating dinosaurs defended themselves against predators in different ways. *Euoplocephalus* had body armor to protect itself against attack, and *Styracosaurus* had large horns that it could use as weapons. Smaller meat-eaters like *Troodon* hunted in packs to bring down prey.

Styracosaurus

Pachycephalosaurus

Parasaurolophus

Euoplocephalus

Troodon

Parasaurolophus

Cretaceous Tyrannosaur: Daspletosaurus

This massive, meat-eating tyrannosaur was a fierce hunter. It had short, deep jaws, which held teeth that were larger than other tyrannosaurs. Each tooth was as sharp as a knife, curved, and had an edge like a saw. Along with its jaws, it used two sets of terrible claws as weapons for slashing open the flesh of prey. *Daspletosaurus* weighed up to 4 U.S. tons (3.6 tonnes). It could kill many of the large, horned dinosaurs that lived in the forests of northern North America at the time. Because it was so big, it probably hunted by hiding amongst the huge trees that grew during the Cretaceous period and ambushing its prey.

Cretaceous Duckbilled Dinosaur: Corythosaurus

Like other "duckbilled" dinosaurs, *Corythosaurus* probably lived in a herd, browsing in the forests for food. *Corythosaurus* had a large fan-shaped crest on top of its head that stood about 1 ft (30 cm) high. Hollow passages, through which *Corythosaurus* breathed, ran up into the crest and looped back down into the snout. It may have used these passages to make sounds, like the pipe of a trombone, to make sounds, like the pipe of a trombone, to communicate with other members of the herd.

Daspletosaurus

Maiasaura

Corythosaurus

Duckbilled Dinosaurs

uckbilled dinosaurs are scientifically known as hadrosaurs. They were a very successful group of dinosaurs that lived across most of the world during Cretaceous times. Hadrosaurs could look quite different from one another. However, they all had a broad, flattened snout with a toothless beak. This beak looked rather like the bill of a modern duck, which is why they have the name of "duckbilled" dinosaurs. There were no teeth in the front of a hadrosaur's mouth. Instead there were rows of cheek teeth. New teeth continually grew to replace old ones that had been worn down or damaged by their tough plant diet.

Tr	Late Triassic
Size: 30 ft/9 m long	
Order: Ornithischia	
Family: Hadrosauridae	
Range: North America: Alberta, Montana, and New Mexico	
Pronunciation: KRITE-oh-SAW-rus	

Bactrosaurus

The earliest-known hadrosaur was *Bactrosaurus*. Paleontologists think that it could have evolved from the iguanodont family. It is one of the smallest duckbilled dinosaurs. It had a low, flat head with no crest, and a narrow bill. The cheek teeth were set well back in the mouth and were perfect for grinding up tough plant material.

Kritosaurus

Kritosaurus had a large, bony hump on its snout in front of the eyes. It is possible that only male *Kritosaurus* had this hump and that it was used to attract females, or to protect the skull in head-butting battles with other males. The males would fight to decide who would lead the herd.

Cr	Late Cretaceous
Size: 13 ft/4 m long	
Order: Ornithischia	
Family: Hadrosauridae	
Range: Asia: Mongolia and China	
Pronunciation: bac-troh-SAW-rus	

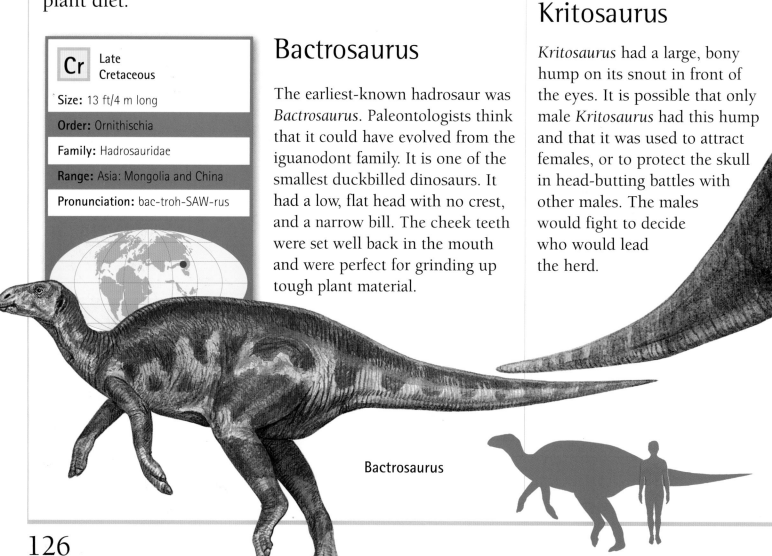

Bactrosaurus

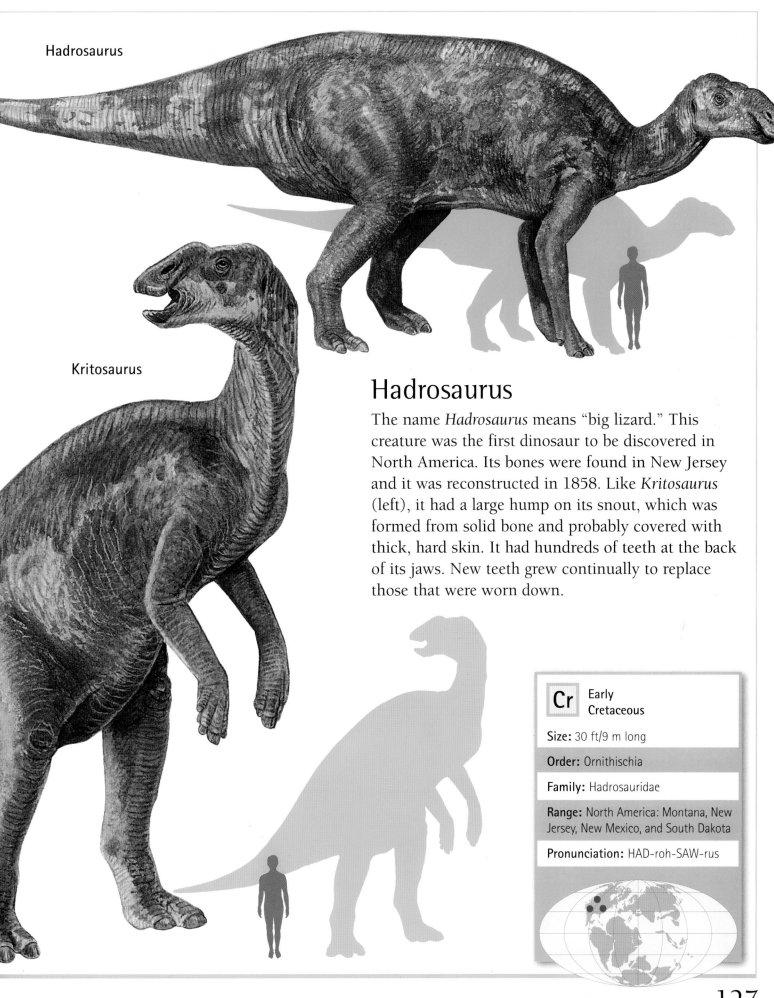

Hadrosaurus

Kritosaurus

Hadrosaurus

The name *Hadrosaurus* means "big lizard." This creature was the first dinosaur to be discovered in North America. Its bones were found in New Jersey and it was reconstructed in 1858. Like *Kritosaurus* (left), it had a large hump on its snout, which was formed from solid bone and probably covered with thick, hard skin. It had hundreds of teeth at the back of its jaws. New teeth grew continually to replace those that were worn down.

Cr	Early Cretaceous

Size: 30 ft/9 m long

Order: Ornithischia

Family: Hadrosauridae

Range: North America: Montana, New Jersey, New Mexico, and South Dakota

Pronunciation: HAD-roh-SAW-rus

Maiasaura

Maiasaura

In 1978 paleontologists found a complete *Maiasaura* nesting site in Montana. The find included the skeleton of an adult, several young dinosaurs, and fossilized nests and eggs. The nests had been made from heaped mounds of mud. Each mound was about 10 ft (3 m) across and 5 ft (1.5 m) high. Mothers probably covered their eggs with earth to keep them warm and protected.

Cr	Late Cretaceous
Size: 30 ft/9 m long	
Order: Ornithischia	
Family: Hadrosauridae	
Range: North America: Montana	
Pronunciation: my-ah-SAW-ra	

Cr	Late Cretaceous
Size: 43 ft/13 m long	
Order: Ornithischia	
Family: Hadrosauridae	
Range: Asia: China	
Pronunciation: shan-TUNG-oh-SAW-rus	

Shantungosaurus

This flat-headed duckbill was one of the largest hadrosaurs. Its extra-long, flat tail made up almost half its total body length. The creature probably weighed over 5 U.S. tons (4.5 tonnes), and used its tail to keep its heavy body balanced when it walked.

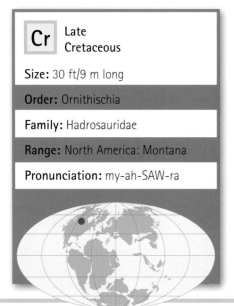

Shantungosaurus

Anatosaurus

Anatosaurus, which means "duck lizard," was named for its horny, toothless bill or beak. It appears to have had webs of skin between the fingers of each hand. At first, paleontologists thought these creatures used their hands for swimming. They now believe that *Anatosaurus* was a land-dwelling dinosaur and that the webs of skin are the remains of walking pads.

Cr	Late Cretaceous
Size: 33 ft/10 m long	
Order: Ornithischia	
Family: Hadrosauridae	
Range: North America: Alberta	
Pronunciation: an-at-oh-SAW-rus	

Anatosaurus

Prosaurolophus

Cr	Late Cretaceous
Size: 26 ft/8 m long	
Order: Ornithischia	
Family: Hadrosauridae	
Range: North America: Alberta	
Pronun: PRO-sore-oh-LOAF-us	

Prosaurolophus

Prosaurolophus' skull was like that of a flat-headed duckbill, such as *Anatosaurus* (above), but it had a solid, bony crest on its head. The crest ran from the tip of the broad snout to the top of the head. It ended in a small, bony knob.

129

Cr	Late Cretaceous
Size: 33 ft/10 m long	
Order: Ornithischia	
Family: Hadrosauridae	
Range: Asia: China	
Pronunciation: SIN-tow-SAW-rus	

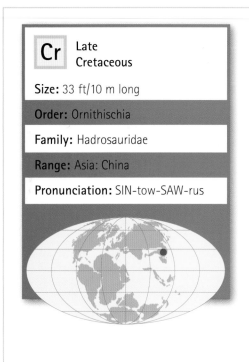

Hypacrosaurus

Hypacrosaurus had a crest on its head that sloped upward in a gentle curve. There was also a large skin-covered ridge down its back. This ridge may have been used to control the animal's body temperature, giving off heat when *Hypacrosaurus* was too hot, and attracting heat if it was too cold. Tracks made by *Hypacrosaurus* have been discovered that suggest it usually walked on four legs.

Cr	Late Cretaceous
Size: 9 ft/30 m long	
Order: Ornithischia	
Family: Hadrosauridae	
Range: North America: Alberta	
Pronun: hie-PAK-roe-SAW-rus	

Hypacrosaurus

Tsintaosaurus

A horn grew from the top of this dinosaur's head, giving it a very unusual appearance. The tip of this horn may have been covered with a flap of skin. This flap could have been inflated like a balloon and used to make signals to other dinosaurs. It may have also been brightly colored.

Tsintaosaurus

Lambeosaurus

Lambeosaurus had two unusual bumps on its head. A tall, hollow crest grew upward from the front of the head and pointed forward. A solid, bony spike grew from the top of the head and pointed backward. *Lambeosaurus* moved around on all fours, and its long, flexible neck meant it could reach low-growing plants easily.

Cr	Late Cretaceous

Size: 30 ft/9 m long

Order: Ornithischia

Family: Hadrosauridae

Range: North America: Baja California, Montana, and Saskatchewan

Pronunciation: LAM-bee-oh-SAW-rus

Lambeosaurus

Parasaurolophus

This duckbill had a hollow, backward-pointing, hornlike crest on the top of its head that was about 6 ft (1.8 m) long. Paleontologists think that *Parasaurolophus* fitted this crest into a notch on its back when it ran through the forest. The crest would sweep any low hanging branches upward and away from the body.

Cr	Late Cretaceous

Size: 30 ft/9 m long

Order: Ornithischia

Family: Hadrosauridae

Range: North America: Alberta, New Mexico, and Utah

Pronun: par-a-SORE-oh-LOAF-us

Parasaurolophus

Feathered Dinosaurs?

During the late 1990s, paleontologists in China uncovered one of the most exciting dinosaur discoveries ever. Several specimens of dinosaurs were unearthed that had the remains of feathers covering parts of their bodies. The discovery suggested that many more dinosaurs had feathers than was first thought. It also gave weight to the idea that modern birds evolved from dinosaur ancestors. But these early feathers were softer and downier than those found on most modern birds, so they were not used for flight.

This fossil was found in 1998 in China. It shows the remains of feather-like structures. This feathered dinosaur lived in the Cretaceous period.

Body covered with downy feathers for warmth

Velociraptor

Early Feathers

The bones of the feathered dinosaurs discovered in China showed that these creatures could not fly—so paleontologists wondered what their feathers were used for. The type of feather was soft and downy, rather than strong like the wing feathers of modern birds. The feathers would have probably been used to keep the dinosaurs warm.

Like the Chinese dinosaurs, modern flightless birds, such as the ostrich, use their feathers to keep warm and for display when attracting a mate.

132

The Earliest Bird

The discovery of *Archaeopteryx* in 1861 was an important find. The fossil had features that linked it with both reptiles and birds. It had the long running legs, bony tail, and clawed fingers seen on many dinosaurs, but impressions of wing feathers had also been preserved in the rock. Its collar bones also formed a birdlike wishbone.

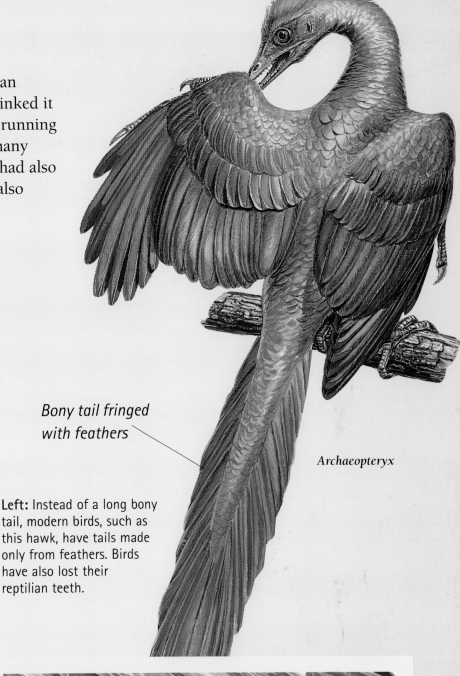

Bony tail fringed with feathers

Archaeopteryx

Left: Instead of a long bony tail, modern birds, such as this hawk, have tails made only from feathers. Birds have also lost their reptilian teeth.

Modern Feathers

Many of the feathers on modern birds are made up of a central shaft to which are attached thousands of barbs. These barbs have tiny hooks called barbules. These link together with the barbules on neighboring barbs to make a smooth and strong surface. This helps to make a bird's body slip easily through the air, allowing it to fly. Feathers found on dinosaurs were without barbules, making them soft and fluffy instead.

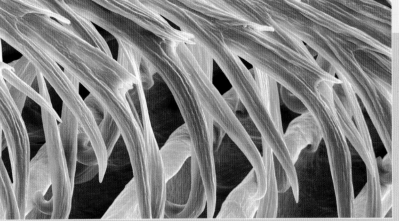

Seen under a microscope, the hooklike structure of the barbules can be seen. They lock into place with barbules on the neighboring barbs of the feather.

Stegosaurs

Ju Late Jurassic

Size: 16 ft/9 m long

Order: Ornithischia

Family: Stegosauridae

Range: Africa: Tanzania

Pronunciation: KEN-tro-SAW-rus

The stegosaurs had a unique appearance. They had small heads but massive bodies. A double row of wide, bony plates ran down each side of their backbones and their heavy tails were armed with pairs of long, sharp spikes. The stegosaurs were plant-eaters and probably lived in herds. They moved about on four legs and were not agile creatures. Unlike quicker dinosaurs, who could run away from predators, stegosaurs relied on their body armor to defend themselves. When attacked, they would most likely have stood their ground, lashing out with their spiked tails and protected by the bony plates on their backs.

Kentrosaurus

Stegosaurus

Ju Late Jurassic

Size: 30 ft/9 m long

Order: Ornithischia

Family: Stegosauridae

Range: North America: Colorado, Oklahoma, Wyoming, and Utah

Pronunciation: STEG-oh-SAW-rus

Stegosaurus weighed up to 2 U.S. tons (1.8 tonnes). Its massive body sloped forward from its highest point at the hips. Wide, bony plates on its back stood up to 2 ft (60 cm) tall, and the spikes on its tail were about 3 ft 3 in (1 m) long.

Kentrosaurus

Kentrosaurus had a double row of narrow, triangular, bony plates that rose on either side of the backbone. Halfway along the back, the plates became pairs of vicious sharp spikes, which ran to the tip of the tail. Some of these spikes were about 2 ft (60 cm) long.

Stegosaurus

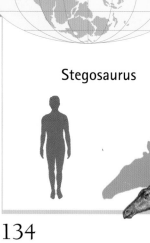

Tuojiangosaurus

Tuojiangosaurus was the first stegosaur to be found in Asia. Its body shape is similar to *Stegosaurus* (far left)—it had a small, narrow head with a large body. Fifteen pairs of bony plates covered its back. These became taller and more spikelike over the hips and down the tail. Like *Stegosaurus*, it had two pairs of long spikes on the tail.

Ju	Late Jurassic
Size: 23 ft/7 m long	
Order: Ornithischia	
Family: Stegosauridae	
Range: Asia: China	
Pronun: toh-HWANG-oh-SAW-rus	

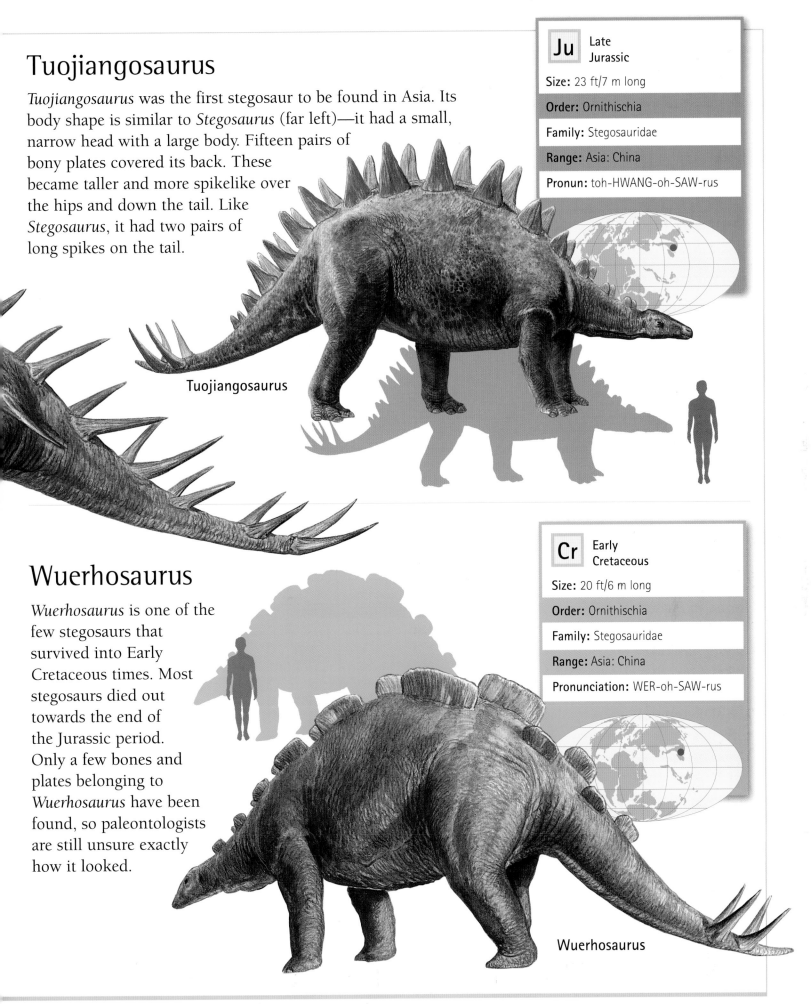

Tuojiangosaurus

Wuerhosaurus

Wuerhosaurus is one of the few stegosaurs that survived into Early Cretaceous times. Most stegosaurs died out towards the end of the Jurassic period. Only a few bones and plates belonging to *Wuerhosaurus* have been found, so paleontologists are still unsure exactly how it looked.

Cr	Early Cretaceous
Size: 20 ft/6 m long	
Order: Ornithischia	
Family: Stegosauridae	
Range: Asia: China	
Pronunciation: WER-oh-SAW-rus	

Wuerhosaurus

135

Nodosaurs

Toward the end of the Jurassic period, stegosaurs began to die out. At the same time, another group of dinosaurs, the ankylosaurs, began to flourish. The nodosaurs were a family of dinosaurs that belonged to this group. They ranged throughout the northern hemisphere during the Cretaceous period, and some types have also been discovered in the southern hemisphere. Like the stegosaurs, the nodosaurs were heavy, four-legged plant-eaters. They had long, narrow skulls, long spikes that stuck out from their sides, and bony plates all over their bodies. These plates were covered in thick, leathery skin and horn, and protected nodosaurs from attack.

Hylaeosaurus

Hylaeosaurus is the earliest known nodosaur. Its remains were first found in Sussex in southern England in the late 1820s. To this day, its fossilized bones are still imprisoned in a slab of rock. There are now plans to remove the skeleton with the use of a chemical called acetic acid. This dissolves the minerals that hold the rock together to release the skeleton inside.

Cr Early Cretaceous

Size: 20 ft/6 m long

Order: Ornithischia

Family: Nodosauridae

Range: Europe: England

Pronunciation: hy-lee-oh-SAW-rus

Polacanthus

Some paleontologists think that *Polacanthus* and *Hylaeosaurus* (below) are the same animals. Only the sturdy back legs and some solid armor plates and spines of *Polacanthus* have been found. Pairs of the heavy spines stood up on the shoulders and upper back, and a shield of bone covered the hips.

Cr Early Cretaceous

Size: 13 ft/4 m long

Order: Ornithischia

Family: Nodosauridae

Range: Europe: England

Pronunciation: pol-a-KAN-thus

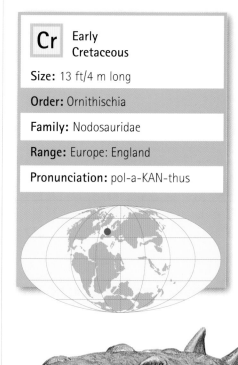

Polacanthus

Sauropelta

Hylaeosaurus

Sauropelta

Sauropelta is the largest
known nodosaur and is thought to have weighed over
3 U.S. tons (2.7 tonnes). Its massive body was covered in
a strong, bony armor. Flexible, horn-covered plates ran
over the body from the neck to the end of the long,
tapering tail. A row of sharp spikes stuck out from
each side to protect *Sauropelta* from attack.

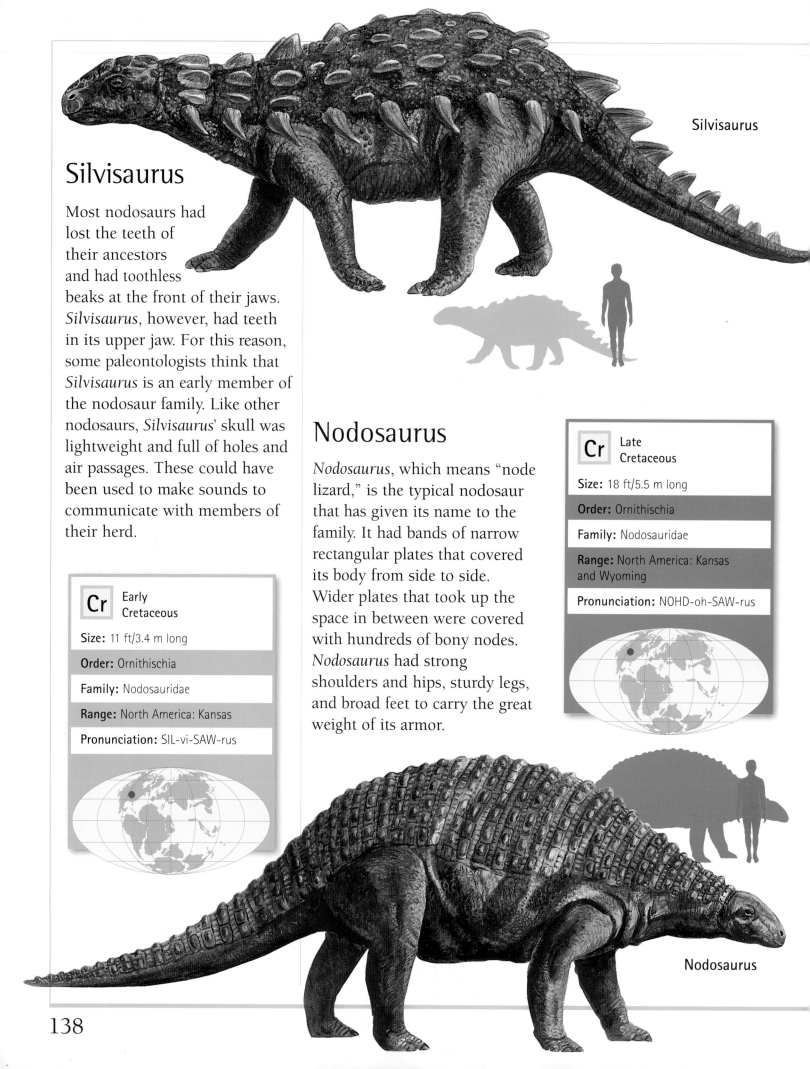

Silvisaurus

Silvisaurus

Most nodosaurs had lost the teeth of their ancestors and had toothless beaks at the front of their jaws. *Silvisaurus*, however, had teeth in its upper jaw. For this reason, some paleontologists think that *Silvisaurus* is an early member of the nodosaur family. Like other nodosaurs, *Silvisaurus*' skull was lightweight and full of holes and air passages. These could have been used to make sounds to communicate with members of their herd.

Cr	Early Cretaceous
Size: 11 ft/3.4 m long	
Order: Ornithischia	
Family: Nodosauridae	
Range: North America: Kansas	
Pronunciation: SIL-vi-SAW-rus	

Nodosaurus

Nodosaurus, which means "node lizard," is the typical nodosaur that has given its name to the family. It had bands of narrow rectangular plates that covered its body from side to side. Wider plates that took up the space in between were covered with hundreds of bony nodes. *Nodosaurus* had strong shoulders and hips, sturdy legs, and broad feet to carry the great weight of its armor.

Cr	Late Cretaceous
Size: 18 ft/5.5 m long	
Order: Ornithischia	
Family: Nodosauridae	
Range: North America: Kansas and Wyoming	
Pronunciation: NOHD-oh-SAW-rus	

Nodosaurus

Struthiosaurus

Cr	Late Cretaceous

Size: 6 ft 6 in/2 m long

Order: Ornithischia

Family: Nodosauridae

Range: Europe: Austria, France, Hungary, and Romania

Pronunciation: STROOTH-ee-oh-SAW-rus

Struthiosaurus is the smallest known member of the nodosaur family. Some scientists think it may have evolved on islands. Many large animals develop dwarf species when they are confined to islands. Food can be scarce on an island, and huge animals cannot find enough to eat to survive.

Struthiosaurus

Panoplosaurus

Panoplosaurus could have weighed as much as 4 U.S. tons (3.6 tonnes). Its heavy body armor was made up of broad, square plates arranged in wide bands across the neck and shoulders. The rest of the back was covered in smaller, bony studs. Massive spikes protected each side of its body. It had a narrow snout and probably rooted among small plants for food.

Cr	Late Cretaceous

Size: 15 ft/4.5 m long

Order: Ornithischia

Family: Nodosauridae

Range: North America: Alberta, Montana, and South Dakota

Pronunciation: pano-o-ploe-SAW-rus

Panoplosaurus

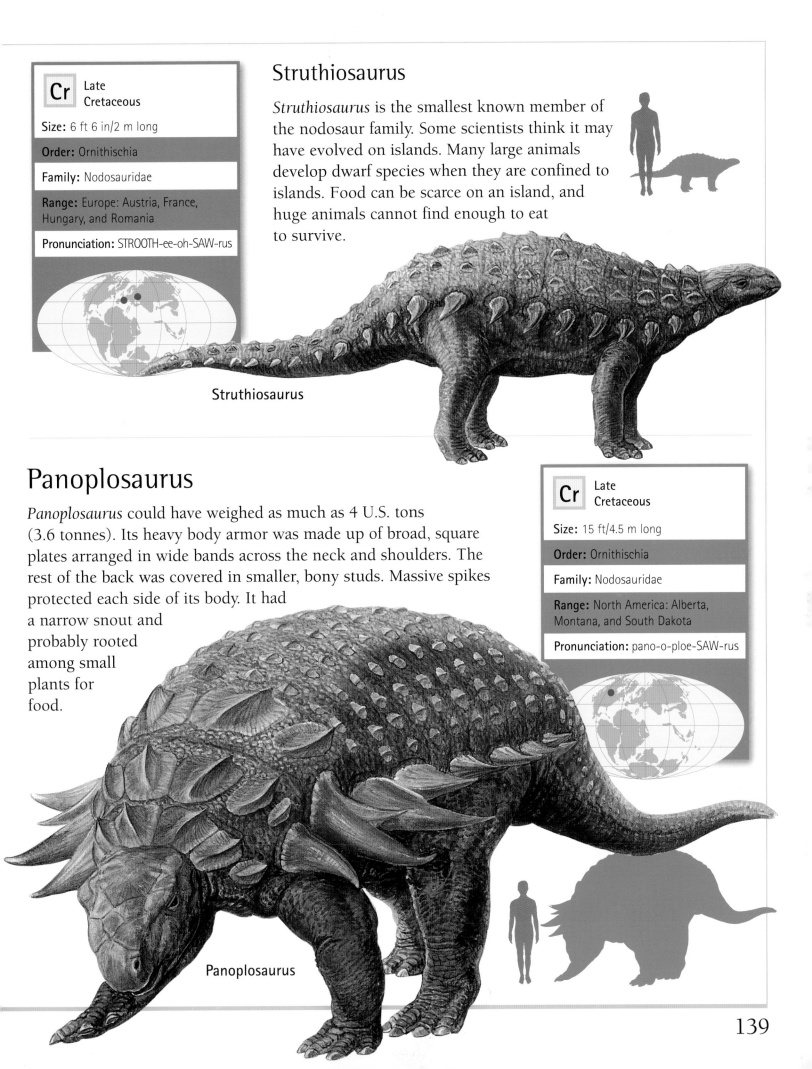

Ankylosaurs

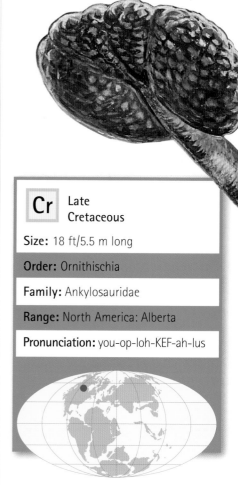

Ankylosaurs thrived toward the end of the Cretaceous period. These plant-eating dinosaurs largely replaced their relatives, the nodosaurs, in western North America and East Asia. Ankylosaurs were shorter and stockier than nodosaurs. They were built like military tanks, and some species were about the same size! They had massive hips and legs to support their heavy bodies. Like the nodosaurs, they had thick plates and spikes on their backs, but the armor on their heads was much more developed. They also had a unique weapon at the tip of their tails—a large ball of bone that could be swung from side to side like a club to kill an attacker.

Cr Late Cretaceous	
Size: 18 ft/5.5 m long	
Order: Ornithischia	
Family: Ankylosauridae	
Range: North America: Alberta	
Pronunciation: you-op-loh-KEF-ah-lus	

Talarurus

Cr Late Cretaceous	
Size: 16 ft/5 m long	
Order: Ornithischia	
Family: Ankylosauridae	
Range: Asia: Mongolia	
Pronunciation: tal-a-ROO-rus	

Talarurus' skull widened at the back to form a pair of bony spikes, which looked like ears. Another pair of spikes stuck out from the cheeks. There was a toothless beak at the front of the jaws and small weak teeth in the back. The body was armored with thick plates and more spikes stuck out from the animal's sides.

Euoplocephalus

Euoplocephalus' head was a heavy box of bone, covered in thick plates. Thick spines protected the sides of the face. Even the eyelids were armored, to guard the eyes like shutters when the animal was under attack. There was a horny, toothless beak at the front of its wide face. *Euoplocephalus* used this for chopping up plant food.

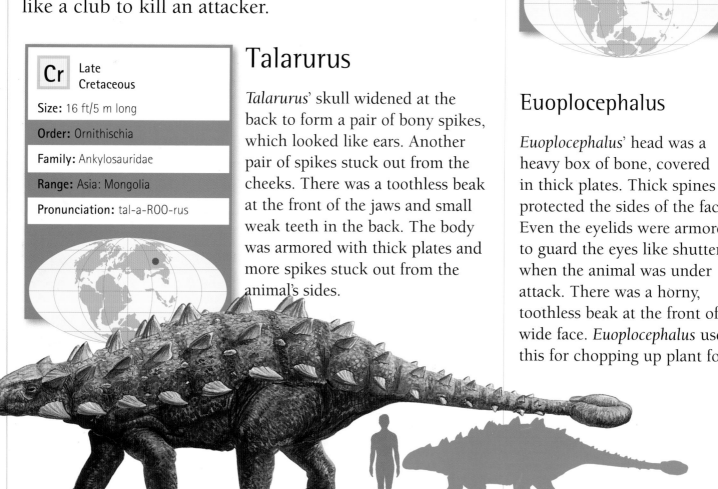

Talarurus

Euoplocephalus

Saichania

The massive head of *Saichania* was armored with great bony nodules. Spikes stuck out from each side of its body. The whole of the back and tail were protected by rows of knobbly plates. *Saichania* probably lived in a hot, dry place where it fed off tough desert plants and grasses.

Saichania

Cr	Late Cretaceous

Size: 23 ft/7 m long

Order: Ornithischia

Family: Ankylosauridae

Range: Asia: Mongolia

Pronunciation: sy-kahn-ee-a

Life in Cretaceous North America

At the end of the Cretaceous period, the dinosaurs and many other creatures disappeared forever. Some paleontologists think they died out when a meteorite collided with the Earth 65 million years ago. But fossils found in North America that date back to this time suggest that dinosaurs were already declining when the meteorite hit.

By comparing the number of fossils found in two different places in North America, paleontologists have learned that the dinosaurs were beginning to disappear toward the end of the Cretaceous period. Fossils that date back 75 million years were discovered in the rocks of the Judith River in Alberta, Canada. From these skeletons, paleontologists could identify 32 different kinds of dinosaurs. In the younger rock of Hell Creek in Montana, which dates back 65 million years, only 19 kinds of dinosaur fossils were found. This drop in numbers could mean that dinosaurs were already starting to die out before the meteorite hit the Earth.

Toward the end of the Cretaceous period in North America, animals lived in a lush landscape of rivers and swamps. *Triceratops*, the armored *Ankylosaurus*, and *Parasaurolophus* were all plant-eaters. The giant pterosaur *Quetzalcoatlus* had a wingspan of 40 ft (12 m). None of these animals survived into Tertiary times, but many mammals did.

Palaeoryctes

Quetzalcoatlus

Triceratops

Albertosaurus

Ankylosaurus

Cretaceous Armored Dinosaur: Ankylosaurus

Ankylosaurus was one of the last armored dinosaurs to survive to the end of the Cretaceous period. It was the largest ankylosaur and probably weighed 4 U.S. tons (3.6 tonnes). Its massive body was 16 ft (5 m) across at the widest point, and it had strong, stumpy legs to support its body's great weight. Thick bands of heavy armor ran across its back from the top of the head to the tip of the tail.

Cretaceous Duckbilled Dinosaur: Edmontosaurus

Many skulls of this large, flat-headed duckbill have been found. It had a toothless beak, but behind this its jaws were packed with teeth—there may have been more than 1,000. These would have been able to grind up even the toughest of plants. *Edmontosaurus* also had a long tail that helped it keep balanced when it stood up on its back legs to run. The tail could also have been used for swimming.

Lambeosaurus

Edmontosaurus

Presbyornis pervetus

Horned Dinosaurs

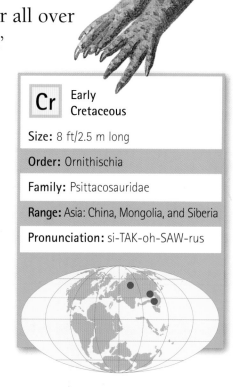

Psittacosaurus

This group of creatures, also known as the ceratopsians, emerged just before dinosaurs became extinct at the end of the Mesozoic era. The ceratopsians lived for 20 million years throughout western North America and central Asia. They were well-armored, but unlike the ankylosaurs who had bony plates of armor all over their bodies, the ceratopsians' weapons only covered their heads. They had massive skulls, with sharp, parrot-like beaks at the front. Long, pointed horns grew from the forehead or snout and a great sheet of bone, called a "frill," grew from the back of the skull and curved upward to protect the neck and shoulders.

Horned dinosaurs were successful because of their excellent chopping teeth and powerful jaws. These dinosaurs could eat even the toughest of plant food. Ceratopsians probably lived in herds in the forests, sticking together for protection. They would browse on low-growing trees and shrubs.

Cr	Early Cretaceous
Size: 8 ft/2.5 m long	
Order: Ornithischia	
Family: Psittacosauridae	
Range: Asia: China, Mongolia, and Siberia	
Pronunciation: si-TAK-oh-SAW-rus	

Psittacosaurus

Psittacosaurus may have been an ancestor of the ceratopians. It had a horny, toothless jaw like a parrot and a thick ridge of bone that ran along the top of the skull. Over millions of years this ridge may have developed into the bony "frill" of later ceratopsians. *Psittacosaurus* had a long flexible neck, four blunt claws on each hand, long back legs, and short front legs.

144

Microceratops

This creature is the smallest horned dinosaur known. *Microceratops* was a lightly-built, two-legged runner. Its front legs, however, were quite long when compared to other two-legged dinosaurs. It probably moved about mainly on four legs, only standing upright to escape from danger.

Microceratops

Cr	Late Cretaceous
Size: 24 in/60 cm long	
Order: Ornithischia	
Family: Protoceratopsidae	
Range: Asia: China and Mongolia	
Pronunciation: mik-roh-SERRA-tops	

Cr	Late Cretaceous
Size: 7 ft/2.1 m long	
Order: Ornithischia	
Family: Protoceratospidae	
Range: North America: Alberta and Wyoming; Asia: Mongolia	
Pronunciation: LEP-toe-SER-a-tops	

Leptoceratops

Leptoceratops could probably walk on two legs as easily as on four. The hind legs were built for running. The five clawed fingers of each hand could be used to grasp bundles of leaves when eating. The bones at the back of *Leptoceratops'* skull curved upwards into a tall peak—an early sign of the neck frill of later ceratopsians.

Leptoceratops

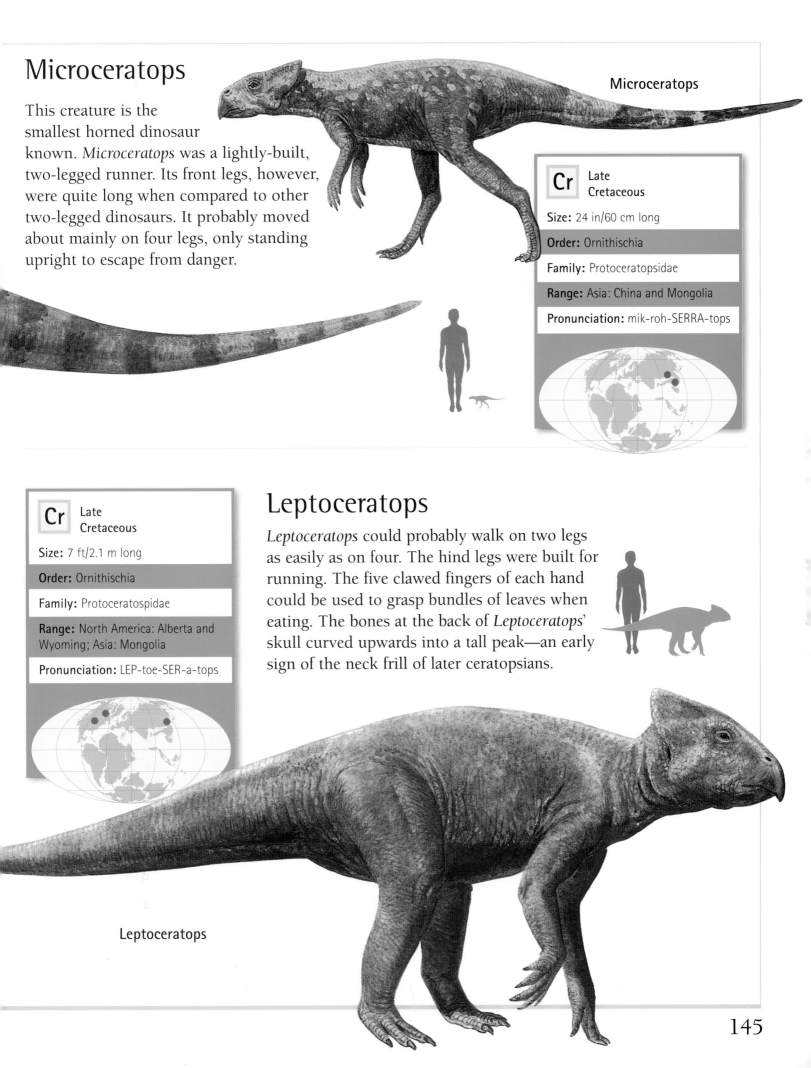

Bagaceratops

Cr	Late Cretaceous
Size: 3.25 ft/1 m long	
Order: Ornithischia	
Family: Protoceratopsidae	
Range: Asia: Mongolia	
Pronunciation: BAG-a-SER-a-tops	

Bagaceratops

Bagaceratops is another possible ancestor of the ceratopsians. This small creature had a squat, heavy body and a long tail. Its sturdy legs were five-toed at the front and four-toed at the back. There was a bony ridge at the back of its skull and a short horn halfway along its snout.

Protoceratops

An adult *Protoceratops* weighed almost 400 lb (180 kg). It had a wide neck frill at the back of its large, heavy skull. Although *Protoceratops* had no horns, it did have a bump on its snout. This bump seems to have been larger in older male creatures. It may have been used for head-butting fights between rival males. *Protoceratops* spent most of its time walking on all-fours, but may have been able to run upright on its back legs.

Cr	Late Cretaceous
Size: 9 ft/2.7 m long	
Order: Ornithischia	
Family: Protoceratopsidae	
Range: Asia: China and Mongolia	
Pronunciation: PRO-toe-SER-a-tops	

Protoceratops

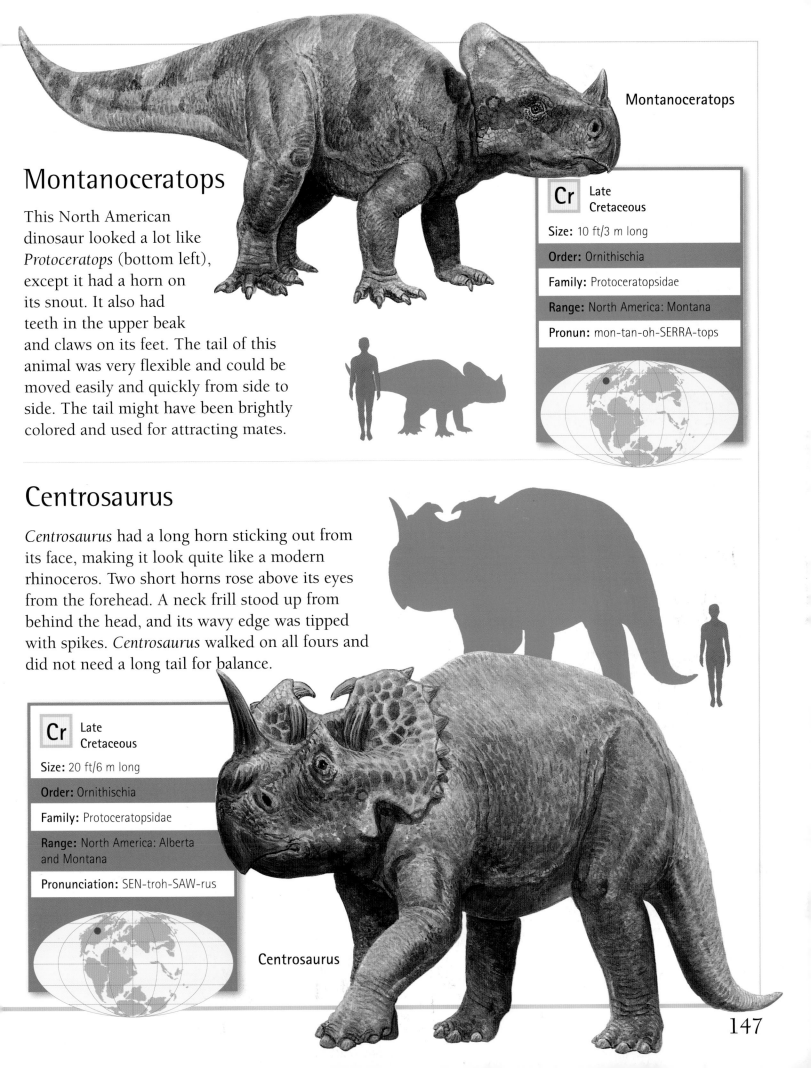

Montanoceratops

This North American dinosaur looked a lot like *Protoceratops* (bottom left), except it had a horn on its snout. It also had teeth in the upper beak and claws on its feet. The tail of this animal was very flexible and could be moved easily and quickly from side to side. The tail might have been brightly colored and used for attracting mates.

Cr	Late Cretaceous
Size:	10 ft/3 m long
Order:	Ornithischia
Family:	Protoceratopsidae
Range:	North America: Montana
Pronun:	mon-tan-oh-SERRA-tops

Centrosaurus

Centrosaurus had a long horn sticking out from its face, making it look quite like a modern rhinoceros. Two short horns rose above its eyes from the forehead. A neck frill stood up from behind the head, and its wavy edge was tipped with spikes. *Centrosaurus* walked on all fours and did not need a long tail for balance.

Cr	Late Cretaceous
Size:	20 ft/6 m long
Order:	Ornithischia
Family:	Protoceratopsidae
Range:	North America: Alberta and Montana
Pronunciation:	SEN-troh-SAW-rus

Centrosaurus

147

Cr	Late Cretaceous
Size: 18 ft/5.5 m long	
Order: Ornithischia	
Family: Ceratopsidae	
Range: North America: Alberta	
Pronun: PAK-ee-RINE-oh-SAW-rus	

Styracosaurus

Styracosaurus was one of the most spectacular of horned dinosaurs. It had an enormous, straight horn on its snout that grew upward and forward. Two smaller horns grew above the eyes. The amazing neck frill had six main spikes around its top, some as large as the nose horn. A number of smaller spikes protected it from attacking predators.

Cr	Late Cretaceous
Size: 17 ft/5.2 m long	
Order: Ornithischia	
Family: Ceratopsidae	
Range: North America: Alberta and Montana	
Pronunciation: sty-RAK-oh-SAW-rus	

Styracosaurus

Pachyrhinosaurus

So far only two skulls of *Pachyrhinosaurus* have been found. Instead of horns it seems to have had a large, thick pad of bone above the eyes. This thick pad may have been used for fighting other dinosaurs in head-butting contests. However, some paleontologists think this pad is scar tissue from where horns fell off.

Pachyrhinosaurus

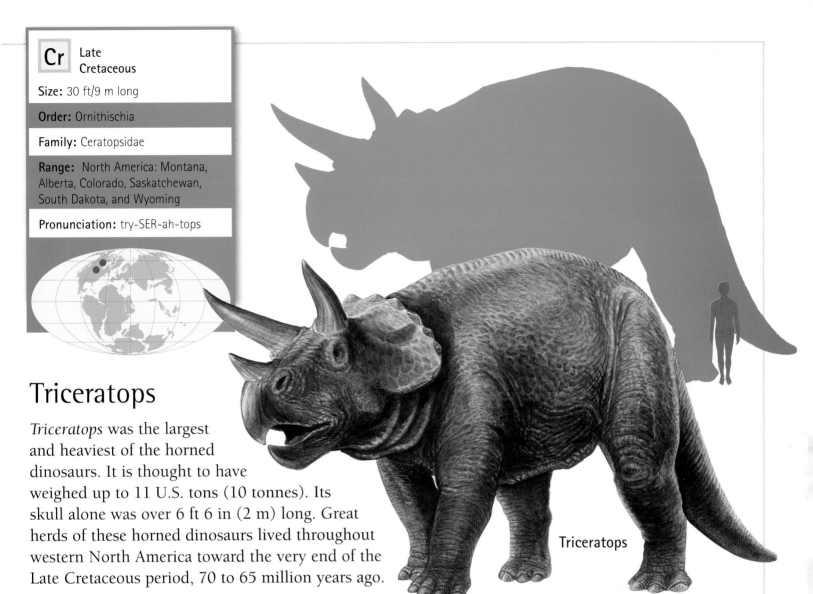

Cr Late
Cretaceous

Size: 30 ft/9 m long

Order: Ornithischia

Family: Ceratopsidae

Range: North America: Montana,
Alberta, Colorado, Saskatchewan,
South Dakota, and Wyoming

Pronunciation: try-SER-ah-tops

Triceratops

Triceratops was the largest
and heaviest of the horned
dinosaurs. It is thought to have
weighed up to 11 U.S. tons (10 tonnes). Its
skull alone was over 6 ft 6 in (2 m) long. Great
herds of these horned dinosaurs lived throughout
western North America toward the very end of the
Late Cretaceous period, 70 to 65 million years ago.

Triceratops

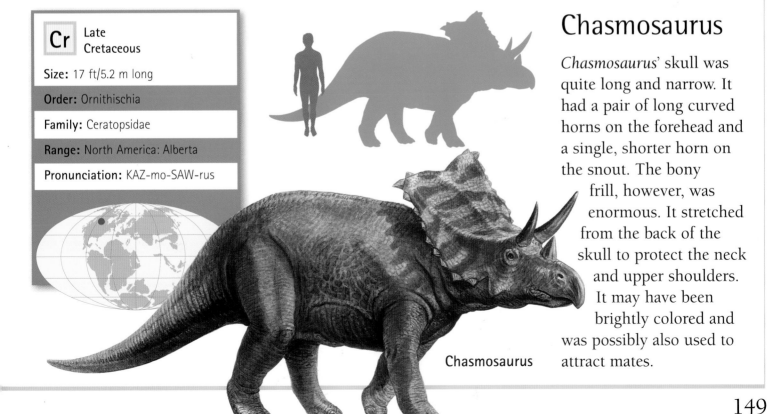

Cr Late
Cretaceous

Size: 17 ft/5.2 m long

Order: Ornithischia

Family: Ceratopsidae

Range: North America: Alberta

Pronunciation: KAZ-mo-SAW-rus

Chasmosaurus

Chasmosaurus' skull was
quite long and narrow. It
had a pair of long curved
horns on the forehead and
a single, shorter horn on
the snout. The bony
frill, however, was
enormous. It stretched
from the back of the
skull to protect the neck
and upper shoulders.
It may have been
brightly colored and
was possibly also used to
attract mates.

Chasmosaurus

149

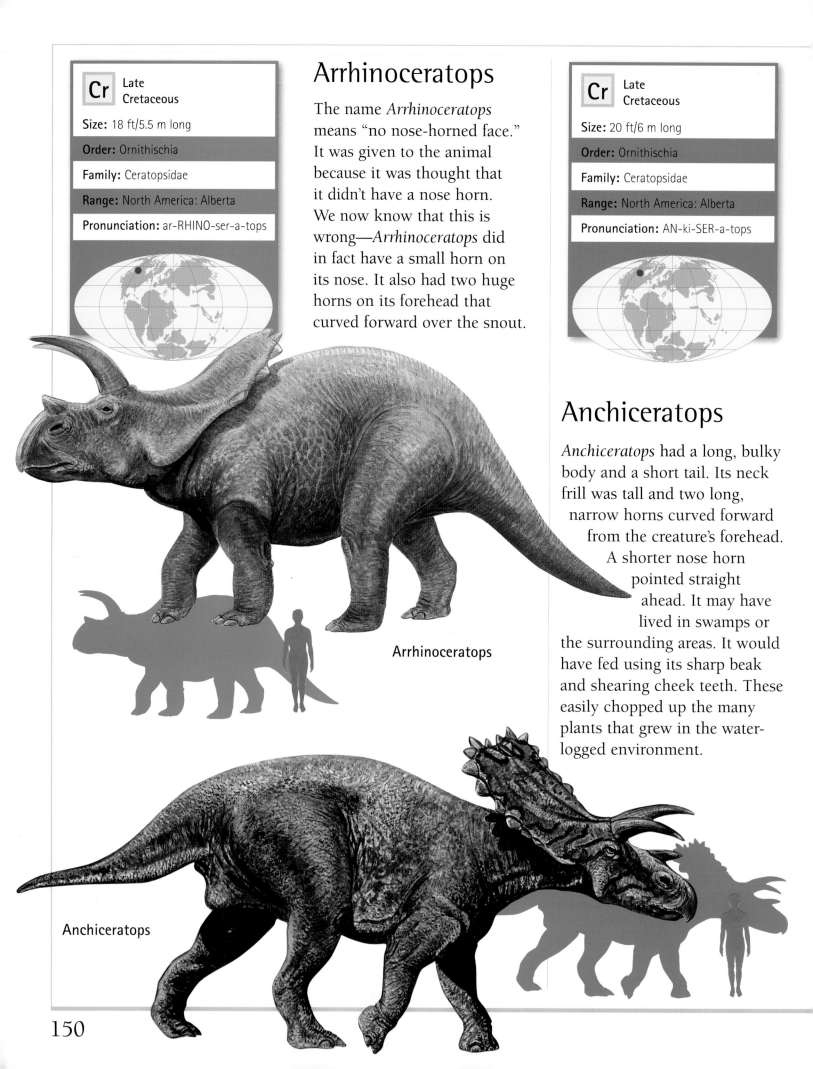

Arrhinoceratops

Cr Late
Cretaceous

Size: 18 ft/5.5 m long

Order: Ornithischia

Family: Ceratopsidae

Range: North America: Alberta

Pronunciation: ar-RHINO-ser-a-tops

The name *Arrhinoceratops* means "no nose-horned face." It was given to the animal because it was thought that it didn't have a nose horn. We now know that this is wrong—*Arrhinoceratops* did in fact have a small horn on its nose. It also had two huge horns on its forehead that curved forward over the snout.

Arrhinoceratops

Anchiceratops

Cr Late
Cretaceous

Size: 20 ft/6 m long

Order: Ornithischia

Family: Ceratopsidae

Range: North America: Alberta

Pronunciation: AN-ki-SER-a-tops

Anchiceratops had a long, bulky body and a short tail. Its neck frill was tall and two long, narrow horns curved forward from the creature's forehead. A shorter nose horn pointed straight ahead. It may have lived in swamps or the surrounding areas. It would have fed using its sharp beak and shearing cheek teeth. These easily chopped up the many plants that grew in the water-logged environment.

Anchiceratops

150

Pentaceratops

Pentaceratops had a huge neck frill with small spines along the edge. When *Pentaceratops* was discovered, scientists thought that they had found an unusual dinosaur with five horns on its face. In fact, *Pentaceratops* had the normal three-horned face: one on its snout and a pair on its forehead. The two extra "horns" were cheek bones that had grown outwards.

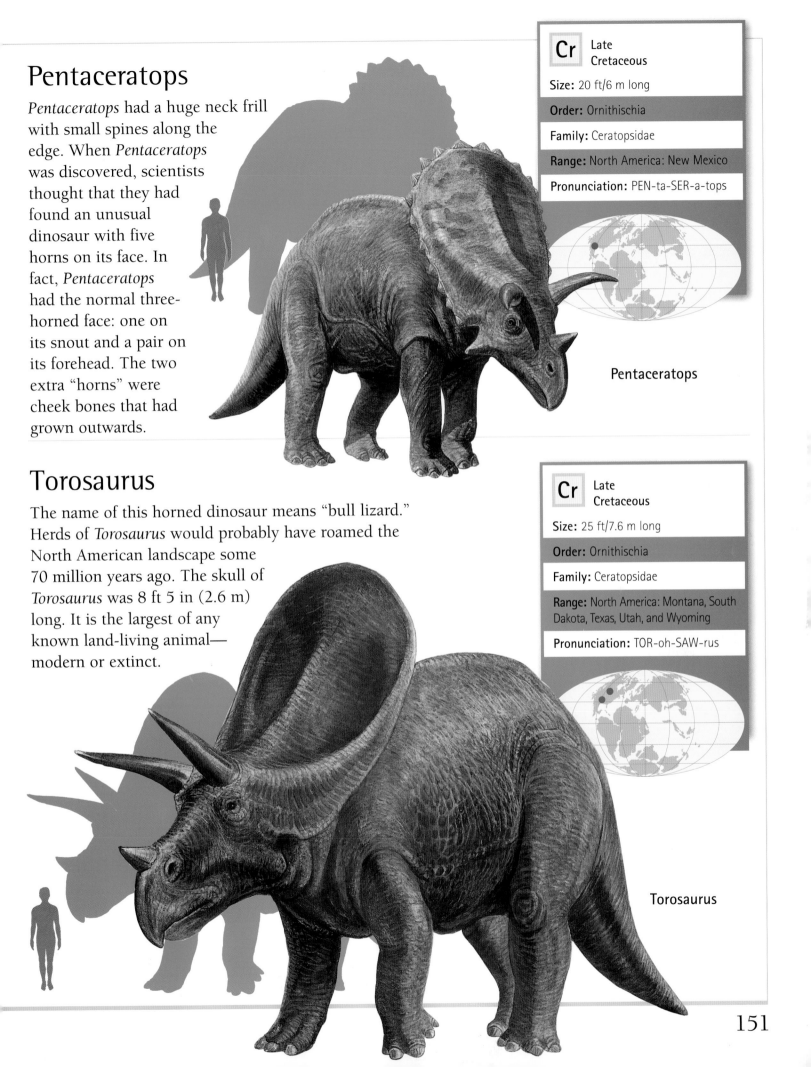

Cr	Late Cretaceous
Size: 20 ft/6 m long	
Order: Ornithischia	
Family: Ceratopsidae	
Range: North America: New Mexico	
Pronunciation: PEN-ta-SER-a-tops	

Pentaceratops

Torosaurus

The name of this horned dinosaur means "bull lizard." Herds of *Torosaurus* would probably have roamed the North American landscape some 70 million years ago. The skull of *Torosaurus* was 8 ft 5 in (2.6 m) long. It is the largest of any known land-living animal—modern or extinct.

Cr	Late Cretaceous
Size: 25 ft/7.6 m long	
Order: Ornithischia	
Family: Ceratopsidae	
Range: North America: Montana, South Dakota, Texas, Utah, and Wyoming	
Pronunciation: TOR-oh-SAW-rus	

Torosaurus

151

The End

No-one knows exactly what caused the death of the dinosaurs and many other creatures about 65 million years ago. Some scientists believe that volcanic eruptions were the cause. Others think the dinosaurs were wiped out by the impact of a huge meteorite from space.

The meteorite would have exploded with the force of thousands of atomic bombs.

Meteorite Impact

A meteorite at least 6 miles (10 km) across hit the Earth 65 million years ago. The explosion would have sent a cloud of dust up into the air, blocking out the Sun's light and warmth. Many plants would have died from lack of sunlight. Plant-eating dinosaurs would have starved to death, followed by the meat-eaters that fed on them.

A massive meteorite crater (seen in this computer-generated image) has been found underwater off the coast of Mexico.

What Died and What Survived?

The dinosaurs were not the only creatures to die out. The flying reptiles—the pterosaurs—also became extinct, as did marine reptiles such as the ichthyosaurs and plesiosaurs. Many life-forms survived, however. Frogs, crocodiles, mammals, snakes, and many insects lived past the Cretaceous period. The extinction of the dinosaurs left a gap for other large animals to fill. Mammals became bigger and more varied until they were the most common large animals on Earth.

While the extinction event 65 million years ago wiped out tens of thousands of different species, many other creatures managed to survive into the Tertiary period.

Reptiles survived

Mammals survived

Plesiosaurs died

Volcanic Eruptions

Even a small volcanic eruption can cause a change in a region's climate. In the Late Cretaceous period there was an enormous amount of volcanic activity. These eruptions would have thrown vast quantities of ash and dust into the air. The ash and dust would have blotted out the sunlight and caused many plants to die. Some scientists believe that the death of the dinosaurs may have been caused by volcanoes, not a meteorite.

Right: Layers of lava from volcanic eruptions in the Cretaceous period formed these rocks in the Deccan region of India.

Quetzalcoatlus

Dromaeosaurus feeding on *Edmontosaurus*

Edmontonia

This scene shows the effect of volcanic eruptions on the climate and wildlife of the Late Cretaceous period. Debris from the volcano has darkened the sky and blocked out the sunlight. Plants are dying out and with them plant-eaters. Meat-eaters survive for a while by eating the bodies.

Triceratops

Pachycephalosaurus

Ammonites died

Dinosaurs died

Amphibians survived

Insects survived

Pterosaurs died

Glossary

ammonite A member of an extinct group of sea-living relatives of today's squid and octopus. An ammonite had a hard, coiled shell, inside which lived a soft-bodied animal with tentacles.

amphibian A four-legged vertebrate animal that can live on land and in water, but usually lays its eggs in water. Modern amphibians include frogs, toads, and salamanders.

archosaur The group of reptiles to which dinosaurs and pterosaurs belong. Crocodiles are the only surviving archosaurs.

beak A mouthpart made of horn on birds and some dinosaurs. Beaks are used in the same way as teeth: to hold on to and chop up food.

billion One thousand million.

boneheaded dinosaurs Dinosaurs with dome-shaped skulls of thickened bone that helped to protect the males during head-to-head fights with other males. There were two groups of boneheads—homalocephalids and pachycephalosaurids.

Carboniferous The period from 360 to 290 million years ago.

carnivore An animal that eats the flesh of other animals in order to survive; a meat-eating creature.

ceratosaurs Meat-eating dinosaurs that walked upright on their back legs and had small front legs. Some ceratosaurs, such as *Ceratosaurus*, had one or more horns on their heads. Others, such as *Dilophosaurus*, had strangely shaped crests.

club moss A type of plant that lived before flowering plants. It was common in the Triassic, Jurassic, and Carboniferous periods, but are now almost extinct.

cold-blooded Used to describe an animal (such as a lizard or a snake) that cannot control its body temperature but must rely on the heat of the Sun to keep it warm.

crest A bony structure on top of the head. It is usually used in display to warn away other males and win a mate.

Cretaceous The period from 146 to 65 million years ago.

cycad A type of cone-bearing plant that lived before flowering plants. Cycads had short thick trunks and long palmlike leaves.

evolution The gradual development of species of plants and animals through time. As plants and animals develop, or evolve, their characteristics change to adapt to their environments.

extinction The death of every single member of a species. Dinosaurs died out and became extinct at the end of the Cretaceous period 65 million years ago.

family A group of related species. For example, all the species of duckbilled dinosaurs, such as *Maiasaura*, belong to the family Hadrosauridae. The scientific name of a family usually ends in -idae.

fossil The remains of an animal preserved in rock. Bones and teeth are more likely to form fossils than soft body parts. Impressions in mud, such as footprints, can also be fossilized.

gastroliths Stones found in the stomachs of some plant-eating dinosaurs to help them break down and digest tough plant food.

ginkgoes Trees that look like conifers but shed their leaves in autumn. The only living species of ginkgo is the maidenhair tree.

Gondwana An ancient landmass that formed when Pangaea broke up about 180 million years ago. Gondwana split to form the southern landmasses of South America, Africa, India, Australia, and Antarctica.

habitat The surroundings in which an animal lives, including the climate, water, and plant life.

hadrosaurs Large plant-eating dinosaurs with long, flat beaks; also called duckbilled dinosaurs. Many hadrosaurs had crests on their heads. Hadrosaurs include *Parasaurolophus* and *Lambeosaurus*.

herbivore An animal that eats plants to survive.

hypsilophodonts Small, lightly built plant eaters that moved upright on their long, slender back legs.

ichthyosaurs Sleek, fast-swimming reptiles that were similar in appearance to dolphins.

iguanodonts Medium- to large-sized plant eaters with hooflike nails on their hind feet and spikes on their hands instead of thumbs, which could be used to fight predators. The fifth finger on each hand could be bent across the palm to grasp food.

Jurassic The period from 208 to 146 million years ago.

Laurasia An ancient landmass formed when Pangaea broke up about 180 million years ago. Laurasia then split to form the northern landmasses of North America and Eurasia.

Laurentia The ancient landmass that consisted of what are now South America, Africa, India, Australia, and Antarctica.

mammal A four-legged vertebrate animal that has hair on its body and feeds its young on milk produced from its own body. Mammals include cats, horses, and humans.

mass extinction The disappearance of a large number of different species over a short period of time.

meteorite A lump of rock from outer space that enters the Earth's atmosphere and lands on Earth.

mosasaur A large, sea-living reptile, closely related to modern lizards.

nodosaurs Armored dinosaurs covered with bony plates, spikes, and knobs.

order A group of related families. There are two orders of dinosaurs—Ornithischia and Saurischia. Orders are divided into smaller groups, called suborders. Suborders are divided still further into infraorders, divisions, and families. For example, *Tyrannosaurus* belongs to the family Tyrannosauridae, the infraorder Tetanurae, the suborder Theropoda and the order Saurischia.

ornithischian dinosaurs Bird-hipped dinosaurs. The Ornithischia order, or group, of dinosaurs includes horned dinosaurs, armored dinosaurs, stegosaurs, and two-footed plant eaters.

palaeontologist A scientist who specializes in the study of fossils and ancient life.

Pangaea An ancient continental landmass that formed about 300 million years ago and included all the world's land. It later split into two parts—Gondwana and Laurasia.

Permian The period from 290 to 250 million years ago.

plesiosaurs Swimming reptiles with paddlelike limbs that lived in the world's seas during the Jurassic and Cretaceous periods.

predator An animal that hunts and kills other animals for food.

prey An animal hunted by a predator.

Quaternary The most recent period of Earth's history, from 1.8 million years ago to the present day.

reptile A four-legged vertebrate animal that lays eggs with tough, leathery shells. Dinosaurs, pterosaurs, and ichthyosaurs were all reptiles. Modern reptiles include tortoises, snakes, lizards and crocodiles.

saurischian dinosaurs Lizard-hipped dinosaurs. The Saurischia order, or group, of dinosaurs includes all the meat-eating theropods and the plant-eating sauropods, or long-necked dinosaurs.

sauropods Long-necked plant eaters, such as *Diplodocus* and *Brachiosaurus*.

scavenger A creature that feeds on the remains of animals that have died naturally or been killed by other flesh eaters.

species A term for a type of plant or animal. Members of the same species can mate and produce young that can themselves have young.

stegosaurs Large plant-eating dinosaurs with rows of triangular plates running down their backs and spikes on their tails.

Tertiary The period from 65 to 1.8 million years ago.

Tetrapods Four-legged vertebrates. Their descendants include amphibians, reptiles, birds, and mammals.

theropod A group of large dinosaurs that were mostly meat eaters and walked on their back legs.

Triassic The period from 250 to 208 million years ago.

vertebra One of the bones that make up a backbone. The backbone is made up of a number of vertebrae.

vertebrate An animal with a backbone. Mammals, birds, reptiles, amphibians, and fish are all vertebrates.

warm-blooded Describes an animal such as a mammal or bird that can control its own body temperature. Most reptiles and amphibians depend on the sun's heat to warm their bodies and are said to be cold-blooded.

Index

Acknowledgments

Artwork credits

t = top; b = bottom; c = center; r = right; l = left

Cover: Steve Kirk

Maps: Eugene Fleury

1c, 1t Steve Kirk; 1b, 2–3 David Bergen; 4–5 Peter David Scott/ Wildlife Art Agency; 7 Steve Kirk; 10–11 Rob Jakeway; 12–13, 14t,14–15, Bill Donohoe; 15t Jim Channell; 16–17, 17t Colin Newman; 18t Steve Kirk; 18b Peter David Scott/Wildlife Art Agency; 18c, 19 Steve Kirk; 20 Peter David Scott/Wildlife Art Agency; 21, 24–25 Steve Kirk; 26–27 David Bergen; 27t, 28–35 Steve Kirk; 36–38 Peter David Scott/Wildlife Art Agency; 36t, 37t, 38–53 Steve Kirk; 54–55 David Bergen; 54t, 55t, 56–61 Steve Kirk; 62–63 Peter David Scott/Wildlife Art Agency; 64–73 Steve Kirk; 74–75 Bill Donohoe; 74t, 75t, 76–81 Steve Kirk; 82 Terry Gabbey/Associated Freelance Artists; 83t Guy Smith/Mainline Designs; 83b, 84–89, 90b, 90–91c Steve Kirk; 91t Peter David Scott/Wildlife Art Agency; 91c, 91b, 92–105 Steve Kirk; 106–107 Peter David Scott/Wildlife Art Agency; 106t, 107t, 108–111, 112–113t, 112–113c Steve Kirk; 112–113b Robin Bouttell; 114–141, 142–143c Steve Kirk; 142–143b David Bergen; 143, 144–151 Steve Kirk; 152tl, 152cr, 152–153c David Bergen; 152–153b Peter David Scott/Wildlife Art Agency.

Photographic credits

b = bottom

8–9 Tony Stone Images; 10 Sinclair Stammers/Science Photo Library; 12 François Gohier/Ardea; 13 Breck P. Kent/Oxford Scientific Films; 16 Zig Leszczynski/Oxford Scientific Films; 22–23 Louie Psihoyos/Corbis; 62–63 Digital Vision Ltd.; 63b Jean-Loup Charmet; 83 Bettmann/Corbis; 132t Reuters/ Corbis; 132b Anup Shah/Nature Picture Library; 133b Andrew Syred/Science Photo Library; 153 E. Hanumantha Rao/NHPA.